Lyndon B. Johnson and

THE OKLAHOMA WESTERN BIOGRAPHIES
RICHARD W. ETULAIN, GENERAL EDITOR

Lyndon B. Johnson
and Modern America

Kevin J. Fernlund

UNIVERSITY OF OKLAHOMA PRESS : NORMAN

Also by Kevin J. Fernlund
William Henry Holmes and the Rediscovery of the American West
(Albuquerque, 2000)
(ed.) *The Cold War American West, 1945 to 1989* (Albuquerque,
1998)

Library of Congress Cataloging-in-Publication Data

Fernlund, Kevin J.
  Lyndon B. Johnson and modern America / Kevin J. Fernlund.
  p. cm. — (Oklahoma western biographies ; v. 25)
  Includes bibliographical references and index.
  ISBN 978-0-8061-4077-3 (cloth)
  ISBN 978-0-8061-6450-2 (paper)
    1. Johnson, Lyndon B. (Lyndon Baines), 1908–1973. 2. Presidents—United
States—Biography. 3. United States—Politics and government—1963–1969.
I. Title.
  E847.F47   2009
  973.923092—dc22
  [B]
                                                           2009005838

Lyndon B. Johnson and Modern America is Volume 25 of The Oklahoma Western
Biographies.

The paper in this book meets the guidelines for permanence and durability of the
Committee on Production Guidelines for Book Longevity of the Council on Library
Resources, Inc. ∞

Contents

Illustrations

Series Editor's Preface

STORIES of heroes and heroines have intrigued many generations of listeners and readers. Americans, like people everywhere, have been captivated by the lives of military, political, and religious figures and intrepid explorers, pioneers, and rebels. The Oklahoma Western Biographies endeavor to build on this fascination with biography and to link it with two other abiding interests of Americans: the frontier and American West. Although volumes in the series carry no notes, they are prepared by leading scholars, are soundly researched, and include a discussion of sources used. Each volume is a lively synthesis based on thorough examination of pertinent primary and secondary sources.

Above all, the Oklahoma Western Biographies aim at two goals: to provide readable life stories of significant westerners and to show how their lives illuminate a notable topic, an influential movement, or a series of important events in the history and cultures of the American West.

Kevin J. Fernlund clearly achieves these major goals in his new study of Lyndon Baines Johnson and the American West. Fernlund's smoothly written book traces Johnson's Texas background and demonstrates how this dynamic place and its shaping forces molded Johnson's early years. The author then deals with Johnson's schooling, teaching, and education administration experiences in Texas before he entered politics. The next chapters treat Johnson's initial roles in Longhorn politics and his first years in the U.S. Congress. Fernlund provides an exceptionally illuminating evaluation of Johnson's adroit political leadership in the U.S. Senate. So successful was this political generalship in the Senate that Fernlund calls Johnson's decision to run for the White House and his eventual acceptance of the vice presidency in 1960–1961 a major mistake. The author's final chapters treat Johnson's ascension to the presidency following the assassination of John F. Kennedy in 1963. These sections deal extensively with Johnson's involvement in the Vietnam War and his Great Society programs. A concluding chapter examines Johnson's lesser-known but central role in the space program. All these discussions clarify how Johnson's Texas and western backgrounds influenced his congressional and presidential actions.

Readers will find Fernlund's book pure pleasure. It moves along smoothly, is well written throughout, and frequently soars. The appealing turns of phrase, fresh expressions, and unusual comparisons will pull in general readers, students, and specialists alike.

Kevin J. Fernlund's new approach to Lyndon Baines Johnson provides a novel reading of this important westerner and his huge circles of influence. The book clearly achieves the major aims of volumes in the Oklahoma Western Biographies series, dealing with a notable person whose life illustrates large happenings in western and national history.

Richard W. Etulain

Preface

MY first public memory is the assassination of John F. Kennedy. I was only a little over four years old on that November day, but I recall distinctly my father coming home from Lowry Air Force Base, where he served as an airman, and immediately upon entering our home in Aurora, Colorado, asking my mother if she had heard the news. Soon we were connected to the rest of the world through our black-and-white television set. I was usually allowed to watch such programs as *Romper Room* and *Captain Kangaroo*, and when the babysitter was over, I watched *Combat, Ben Casey, The Outer Limits*, and *The Red Skelton Show*. But sitting cross-legged in the living room on a large oval-shaped woven rug, which looked like a giant bull's eye, I was introduced that day to continuous news coverage. The journalists were serious and earnest, just like my parents that day. And everything was so sad. The somber tone of it all made a very deep impression on me, as it did on many others. At some point, I saw real-time footage of Lyndon B. Johnson. He was identified as the man who would succeed the slain president. His name meant nothing to me, of course, but his large frame struck me, as did that somber face, burdened with responsibility.

I would see Johnson many times in the ensuing years on the evening news, which we watched regularly in our living room in Tucson, Arizona, after my father was transferred to Davis-Monthan Air Force Base in 1964. Like so many others of that era, I watched the Vietnam War, which I found incomprehensible, slowly unfold on television. And I have memories of going to Swan Park to play army with the other boys from the neighborhood. I vividly recall watching as the blue Arizona sky was sliced up every day into large patches by the white contrails that fighter jets left behind, and hearing the roars and sonic booms these planes made, which rattled the windows. And while I looked up, my father was serving deep underground beneath the cactus and creosote, in a missile silo someplace outside Tucson.

Later I would come to see Johnson as more of a historical figure than a contemporary one. But no matter how detached or objective I became, I could never completely escape that initial childhood impression I had of the man. Later, I realized that his journey as president of the United States started at precisely the same time my journey as an American citizen began, for while I certainly could not have expressed it in just those terms then, it is clear to me now that I became an American on November 22, 1963, and that my sense of national identity is forever associated with that tragic day. That says something about me, I suppose. Thus, this biography is in a real sense personal — as all are — although the subject is in no way about me, of course.

This is a book about the life of Lyndon B. Johnson and the American West, a region he worked hard to personify and the spirit of which he sought to convey. But this book is also very much about Johnson and his times, the remarkable period in U.S. history from 1932 to 1968, years Johnson helped define as much as he was defined by them. So much so, that we can speak of this time as the Age of Johnson.

St. Louis
January 2009

Lyndon B. Johnson and Modern America

CHAPTER I

Headwaters

PLACE matters. And it matters that Lyndon Baines Johnson, the thirty-sixth president of the United States, was born in a farmhouse on the Pedernales River in the oak- and juniper-covered Hill Country of Texas. The Pedernales drains only a portion of the Hill Country, and is in fact tributary to the Colorado. The flood-prone Colorado, in turn, like Texas's other major rivers — the Sabine, the Trinity, the Brazos, and the Rio Grande — follows a southeasterly course down to the Gulf of Mexico. The Colorado arises in the Llano Estacado, or Staked Plains, actually a vast grass-covered mesa shared by New Mexico and Texas. It runs down through the Hill Country, or Edwards Plateau, where it is infused by the Pedernales. The Colorado River flows on past Austin, the state capital and state seat of learning, and across the ninety-eighth meridian — the dividing line between humid and arid America, according to Texas historian and author of *The Great Plains* (1931) Walter Prescott Webb. The Colorado then heads across the coastal plain, before finally emptying into Matagorda Bay. On the river's nearly nine-hundred-mile journey, it cross-cuts both Texas geography and history.

Water was a subject dear to Johnson throughout his long public career, as it was to every right-thinking westerner. Indeed, Johnson would later succeed in helping transform Texas's rivers through dams, reservoirs, and other projects into an elaborate and tolerably well regulated plumbing system. Of course, the Hill Country of Johnson's birth in 1908 had already experienced dramatic changes in the previous century, as Euro-Americans, including Johnson's own ancestors, tried to turn the country into

3

money through enclosure, fire suppression, and grazing. The impact of the market, private capital, and land ownership on nineteenth-century Texas was profound. In many places, however, as in Johnson's Hill Country, the transformative effect of these economic forces was spent after the lucky and enterprising few had raked off fortunes — some greater than others — in cotton, cattle, and lumber. The Hill Country was poorer than most regions — its principal resource amounting to a few inches of topsoil spread out over an uneven tabletop of white chalky limestone — and it was quickly left behind, like a boulder displaced and exposed by a flash flood. For the stickers, those who stayed put and eked out a living in these hills and stunted trees, the post-frontier twilight lasted well into the twentieth century. And it was into this dwindling glow that Johnson first came to know the world.

Three marked strains converged to form the Johnson family: the Buntons, Baineses, and Johnsons. Johnson's genealogy reads like a classic account of Texas history. Indeed, his ancestors were involved in virtually every major episode of the state's storied past, including the Texas Revolution and the American Civil War. John Wheeler Bunton, Johnson's great-great-uncle, who was originally from Tennessee, fought — by all accounts heroically — in the 1835–1836 Texas uprising against Mexico. He also enjoyed the distinction of having signed the Texas Declaration of Independence. The Texas Revolution led to the creation of yet another slave power in North America, before the Lone Star Republic was absorbed nine years later by the much larger and older slave power the United States. Moreover, Bunton turned his battlefield exploits into votes — a time-tested political alchemy — and won a seat in Texas's first congress. He is remembered for writing legislation that established the Texas Rangers, an armed and mounted force tasked with controlling the new nation's non–Anglo American populations, namely Indians and Mexicans.

Bunton soon forsook politics, however, and moved west near Bastrop, a town situated at the Old San Antonio Road crossing of the Colorado River, where he started a plantation with his family and slaves. This was dangerous country, given that the southeastern border of the Comanche raiding and trading empire extended into central Texas, where it now came into bloody conflict with Texas's advancing northwestern frontier. The violence that resulted was intense and unusually prolonged. Indeed, although Comanche power started to decline well before the Mexican War, it was not until 1874 that the U.S. Army was finally able to subjugate "the people" in the 1874 Red River War, a result that was ensured by the destruction of the great southern herd of American bison.

In the half century in between, numerous individual encounters between Indians and whites left hundreds dead on both sides. Despite actually being the tip of the spear, frontier Texans saw the matter very differently. In the stories they told of this contested period, the heroes were the lone homesteader and his family bravely fighting a numerically superior and savage enemy. In this version of events, white settlers were somehow disconnected from the civilization from whence they came. And in a state where not only was slavery legal, but the people (white Texans, anyway) would elect to go to war with the Union to make the South safe for slavery once and for all, the stories of Comanche abductions, especially of white women and children, still elicited a particular horror. Slavery was supposed to be a one-way street, with the traffic in human beings determined by race. The Comanches, however, thought otherwise. Captivity was as common to them as bondage was to southerners.

Johnson's own grandmother Eliza Bunton Johnson, the daughter of John Wheeler Bunton's younger brother, Confederate and rancher Robert Holmes Bunton, and wife of Sam Ealy Johnson, nearly suffered such a fate. Left alone with the children at their Hill Country cabin, Eliza and her little girl, Mary, narrowly escaped detection by a party of Comanche raiders. They did so by hiding in the root cellar. The Comanches took what items they wanted, just as the Johnsons and other Hill Country settlers had earlier helped themselves to Comanche land. The point of the story, of course, was not the brutal quid pro quo at work on the frontier but the real courage of these frontier men and women in the face of great peril. Moreover, such stories of courage and pluck fortified pioneers and inspired their descendants. And it gave them a sense of place that was tougher and deeper than was perhaps true of other Euro-Americans who settled in country less contentious than that of the Pedernales.

Eliza Johnson's husband, like her father, had taken up arms against the United States. Sam saw his share of action on the Texas coast at Galveston Island and along the Red River valley in western Louisiana. He even had a horse shot out from under him while fighting for the cause. And after the war, Sam, like his father-in-law and many other cash-poor ex-Rebels, saw a winning formula in combining the state's feral cattle with its free grass. For a time, Sam and his brother Tom were successful trail drivers, and their dreams of becoming rich selling Texas cattle to their former enemies — Yankee buyers in Kansas — were seemingly realized. But prices eventually fell, and with them the hopes of the Johnson brothers.

The postwar boom in cattle would help set Texas apart from the rest of the South, a region reeling from the consequences of their armed rebellion and the economic and financial shock brought about by the liberation of four million Americans from an institution worth several billion dollars. As a result, the southern economy fell behind and all but became subordinated to northern capital and interests. This sectional shift in power, wealth, and status reflected the obvious: the Confederacy had lost the war, cotton was dethroned, and the United States was becoming an industrial nation and world power. The South's relative economic diminishment as well as its social transformation and subsequent ossification along black and white racial lines defined the region's politics, from the end of the Civil War to the beginning of the civil rights movement a century later.

Texas did not escape the fate of the former Confederate states, of course. Its postwar experience closely paralleled theirs, especially in the cotton country, east of the ninety-eighth meridian. But Texas, unlike the rest of the South, had more to offer the

North's investors and entrepreneurs than just cheap cotton, cheap labor, and low taxes — along with other various and sundry inducements. Besides lots of grass, Texas had vast pools of oil locked underground, which would be tapped by northern industry as the United States shifted from coal to oil in the twentieth century. Indeed the discovery of Texas oil helped propel the shift. The great Spindletop oil strike (near Beaumont, Texas) occurred in 1901, starting an oil rush in which a few Texans became very rich while the rest of American society created a new civilization dependent on high-energy use and cheap fossil fuel. While Johnson's Hill Country was, as it turned out, oil poor, in a state that was otherwise famously oil rich, it did possess grass — and bluebonnets — in abundance, a renewable but soon severely overgrazed resource that Johnson's grandfather Sam and many other Hill Country ranchers exploited, along with all the grass that their herds could eat along the Chisholm Trail. Thus, the economic gloom that settled over the South in the postwar years did not fully extend to central and western Texas, where the new Cattle Kingdom brought hope to thousands and produced a remarkable and long-lived type, the American cowboy. So if there were cotton, slaves, and rebels in Johnson's family history, there were also, in equal measure, grass, cattle, and cowboys — the Old West no less than the Old South.

Johnson's Hill Country was opened to settlement by nineteenth-century market capitalism but failed to progress much past the initial booms in cattle and cotton. There was not even a railroad — in what was an age of railroads — to gouge locals and stir resentment and anger, a commonplace reaction to perceived or real economic discrimination outside the country's industrial core. Indeed, the technological advances, which everywhere in the world had sped up the movement of people, goods, and information, while at the same time reducing the costs of this movement, failed to transform the Hill Country. The farms, ranches, and towns there remained peripheral, if not incidental, to America's modernization and rise as a world power. By the 1880s, many who had fought to divide the Union, including

Sam Ealy Johnson, Sr. (center) with family members, ca. 1893–1897. On his right is his wife, Eliza Bunton Johnson, and to her right is her mother, Priscilla Jane McIntosh Bunton. (LBJ Library, JFC Collection)

Johnson's grandfather Sam, found themselves as much defeated in the marketplace as they had been on the battlefield. Not surprisingly, the Populist revolt against the industrial order at the end of the nineteenth century started in the old Confederate states — in Lampasas, Texas, actually — and spread east from there to the Deep South and west to the plains and the Rocky Mountains.

Populism was a complicated movement, to be sure; it meant different things to different people in different regions and had more than its share of paranoia, if not outright craziness. But at bottom, the Populists were reformers who believed that men should be governed by men, not by abstract economic and global forces. It was a powerful idea, all the more so because it rose out of hard and sometimes bitter experience. In 1892, Sam — by then an old-time drover turned politician — ran as the

Populist candidate for the Texas legislature. He lost soundly, even though other Populists won and carried the district, but passed his politics on to his son, Sam Ealy Johnson, Jr., who was born in Buda, Texas, in 1877. The younger Sam's life would be a struggle. He taught school in the Hill Country, in Sandy and Hye, and cut hair on the side. He raised cotton and fell into debt but won a seat in the state legislature. Sam would pass on his populism, as surely as if it were encoded genetically, to his son, Lyndon; but not before, of course, Lyndon's father had met Lyndon's mother, Rebekah Baines, a young reporter whom Sam married on August 20, 1907.

Since 1904, Rebekah's family had been living in Fredericksburg, a prosperous German community located in the western Hill Country near the Pedernales Valley. Before that, the Baineses had lived in Blanco, where they had moved after a four-year stay in Austin. Rebekah was born in McKinney, Texas, in 1881. Her mother was Ruth Huffman, and her father, Joseph Wilson Baines, was an attorney who had served as secretary of state (1883–1887) under Texas governor John Ireland, and as a legislator from the Eighty-Ninth District. Unfortunately, his financial fortunes never equaled his prominence in the law. Still, Rebekah, who was raised a Baptist, managed to attend Baylor Female College (today's University of Mary Hardin-Baylor) in Belton; men went to Baylor University in Waco. Her grandfather, George Washington Baines, Sr., a Baptist pastor and friend of Sam Houston, had served as president of Baylor University during the Civil War. Rebekah studied literature but did not graduate with a degree. Given her family and religious background, her education, and her appreciation for the finer things, her marriage to Sam Ealy, Jr., despite the promise of youth, in the end perpetuated the same failures to reconcile expectations with reality that had marked her father's experience. This disappointment was defining and goes far to help explain Johnson's own restless youth and lifelong drive for success.

Lyndon Johnson, the first of Rebekah and Sam's five children (the siblings were Rebekah, Josefa, Sam Houston, and Lucia), was born on August 27, 1908, in a farmhouse near the banks of the Pedernales River—not far from Stonewall (in Gillespie County). Stonewall was originally called Millville, but in 1882, following the end of Reconstruction, the small village (population two hundred in 1925) was defiantly renamed after the Confederate general and revered Rebel hero Stonewall Jackson. The tiny community is situated on Highway 290, midway between Fredericksburg to the west and Johnson City to the east. The German immigrants who settled in this area raised both sheep and cattle and experimented with fruit trees, successfully, as it turned out. Indeed, Johnson's birthplace is otherwise famous (and rightly so) for its delicious peaches.

Johnson's very first years were spent on the family farm near Stonewall, and in 1912, at the tender age of four, he attended the nearby Junction School, a one-room structure, which was not unlike something from the artistic imagination of Winslow Homer. Johnson received his first formal instruction from Miss Kathryn Deadrich. This experience, which called to mind the nineteenth century and its frontier schools, McGuffey Readers, and three R's, was brief. In September of the following year, the Johnson family moved east to Johnson City, an old way station and crossroads (today highways 290 and 281 meet here), located fourteen miles away in neighboring Blanco County, just south of the Pedernales River. Named after a relative, James Polk Johnson, the community had served as the county seat since 1890. The town could boast of several stone buildings, giving it a solid, respectable appearance. One of them, the courthouse, built in an attractive, if modest, classical revival style, was not finished until 1916, when Lyndon was eight years old. There might not have been a railroad station in town, directly linking Johnson City with the great American market and the world beyond, but there was a shiny new courthouse. If it was but one of countless other monuments of self-government, dotting the countryside from the Atlantic to the Pacific, it was also a direct cultural link between Johnson City and the civilized world. And this newly constructed edifice, a place of simple dignity, was known well to young Lyndon. It was where locals gathered to

Lyndon B. Johnson, ca. 1915. (LBJ Library)

discuss politics, as if from another painted scene, this one lifted
from the canvas of George Caleb Bingham.

The Johnson family moved into a one-story Folk Victorian,
which was built in 1901 by the Blanco County sheriff, W. C.
Russell, and located close to the center of town. Of course, in a

town as small as Johnson City, everything was relatively close or within walking distance of downtown. Sam Ealy Johnson, Jr., paid $2,925 for the place. This simple, decent, and attractive house had three bedrooms; a kitchen; a dining room; a fireplace; a parlor, which separated the west and east porch; another porch in the back, a good-size sleeping porch, and a tub room. This was the home where Lyndon would grow up.

On May 24, 1924, Lyndon graduated from Johnson City High School. He was fifteen years old. He was quick, and so he got by, but he was not considered a serious student. He craved attention and could be overbearing. Not surprisingly, such a personality bored easily, and Johnson sought out the company and stimulation of those older than him. He was fortunate that his mother was college educated and, to help make ends meet, taught elocution classes at home. (Rebekah also corresponded for several Texas newspapers, including the Johnson City weekly, the *Record Courier*.) But Johnson enjoyed more than this extracurricular formal instruction in the arts of public speaking. He was also schooled in its application. His father was a state legislator (first elected in 1904 to a seat that had been held by his future father-in-law, Joseph Baines). Sam Johnson took his son to Austin to see a lawmaker's life in the capital. And on trips around the Eighty-Ninth District, Johnson saw firsthand his father politicking with Hill Country citizens. In light of Johnson's later career as an orator and a politician, it is impossible not to attach great significance to these early formative experiences.

Although Lyndon's mother was from a long line of Baptists and his father was a late-in-life convert to the Bible-centric Christadelphian Church, founded by John Thomas, Johnson showed, at fourteen, that he was very much of his own mind when he joined the First Christian Church (Disciples of Christ) of Johnson City, a moderate and liberal alternative to the more fundamentalist and purist faiths of his parents. The Disciples emphasized reason in faith and social justice. At a revival meeting, Johnson confessed and was then baptized in the Pedernales River. In 1969, when Johnson's minister, George Davis of National City Christian Church, Washington, D.C., was asked what were Johnson's religious attitudes and convictions, Davis answered, "One of the very outstanding mottos of the leaders of our denomination from the beginning was the motto 'Come let us reason together' [from Isaiah 1:18]. We believed in the rationality of religion." And Davis added, "I wouldn't be surprised if maybe Johnson was influenced by this approach to religion, that religion could be reasonably discussed."

The road from Johnson's boyhood home in Johnson City to the White House years later in retrospect seems remarkably straight. However, there was a notable detour from the "path to power," as Johnson's unsparing biographer Robert A. Caro has called it, following Johnson's high school graduation. Between the time Johnson finished school in 1924 and his enrollment in Southwest Texas State Teachers College in San Marcos (today's Texas State University–San Marcos), three years elapsed. In this period Johnson's future seemed anything but certain. At first, he struck out for California and spent almost a year in San Bernardino, clerking in the law office of his cousin Tom Martin. But Martin turned out to be less than a reliable mentor (according to Caro, he enjoyed partying more than practicing law). It would not be as a lawyer that Johnson would make his mark. He came home out of sorts. He took different odd jobs, including one on a Texas road construction gang, and while he fought a losing battle with small town boredom, he did succeed in causing his parents a good deal of anxiety. It was a relief to everyone, then, especially his mother, when Johnson had enough of drifting and decided to make something of himself and go to college.

San Marcos, located in Hays County, just east of Blanco County, was a town of four thousand souls, with roots extending back to the Spanish colonial era. Like Bastrop, it was a stop on the Old San Antonio Road to Nacogdoches. But it was no ordinary stop. San Marcos, after all, was located along the broken and faulted country — Balcones Escarpment — that lies between Edwards Plateau and the rich black prairies that stretch to the east. Moreover, along the escarpment were clusters of springs, including Barton Springs in Austin's Zilker Park, where folklorist J. Frank Dobie (1888–1964), naturalist Roy Bedichek (1878–1959), and historian Walter Prescott Webb (1888–1963) would famously meet and philosophize, legendary confabs now memorialized in a life-size statue. These lights from the University of Texas gave the study of their state a respectability that it had not previously possessed.

The springs at San Marcos (now known as Aquarena Springs) gushed no less than 200 million gallons a day, from groundwater flow originating in catchment and recharge areas, which surfaced here to form the San Marcos River. Clearly, San Marcos had the capacity, but not unlimited capacity, to grow. Unlike the nearby but nevertheless remote and backward Hill Country, where Johnson grew up, San Marcos, situated as it was on Balcones Escarpment and in the middle of the corridor between San Antonio and Austin, was, if not in the heart of Texas, close enough that this mythical organ could be heard beating from there. And this is where Johnson, with the strong support of his family (support that was perhaps more moral than financial), would spend the next four years — except for a brief but significant interlude as a school principal in Cotulla, a South Texas town on the Nueces (Nuts) River between San Antonio and the border town of Laredo.

In 1927, the same year Charles Lindbergh made his famous flight across the Atlantic, Johnson enrolled for classes. Southwest Texas State Teachers College, which began admitting students in 1903, was housed in a grand Victorian Gothic structure, covered with a striking red roof. This Old Main looked different than it does today, surrounded now by tall trees and other buildings. Built atop Chautauqua Hill, the college in Johnson's day stood alone, looking particularly imposing. The man who ran this institution, Cecil E. Evans, who was educated in Alabama and Texas, had become president in 1911, before Johnson had even started school in Stonewall. (Evans served in this capacity for thirty-one years.) Evans — a man who was as respectable as he was dependable — would make a real difference in Johnson's life. He helped the young Johnson with jobs, even housing.

In contrast to his recent bad-boy period in Johnson City, which followed the sojourn in California, Johnson's college years were filled with a strong and urgent sense of purpose. Making the most of the opportunities presented at Southwest Texas State, Johnson, a history student, signed on as editor of the student newspaper, *The College Star*. In an editorial that he wrote as a freshman on October 5, 1927, perhaps with his mother's help, about "Lucky Lindbergh," the nation's heroic aviator, it is not hard to see that Johnson's comments could have easily been applied to himself. In "He Who Conquers," Johnson unabashedly moralized to his fellow students that

> The adjective which most characteristically describes Lindbergh is not lucky, but plucky. A sketch of his life reveals the grit and determination that have been outstanding traits of his. His was not an easy road. He is a simple, straightforward, plucky lad whose first lesson learned was self-mastery. He did not give up when hardships and trials beset him, but pressed on bravely. . . . It was a wonderful thing to make the first trans-ocean flight. It is a more wonderful thing to conquer self, master life and achieve spiritual independence.

Not everything Johnson wrote was so personally revealing. He was characteristically less transparent and more effusive and saccharine — folks in cattle country might use a more pungent and earthy adjective to describe his writing. For instance, in another editorial, a paean, really, to teaching, entitled "The Greatest of Vocations," Johnson likened the teacher to a Pied Piper who "with his flute charmed the children to a wonderful land beyond." Such sentiment and enthusiasm were, of course, pretty standard fare in teacher preparation programs, then no less than now. At the very least, his editorials showed a student who fully and early on grasped a cardinal principle of communication — know your audience.

By all accounts, Johnson's academic record proved less than distinguished, even if he formed close relationships with his professors, including the eccentric and colorful H. M. Greene, who taught that government ought to protect the poor from the rich. Unfortunately in life, there are few points awarded for overcoming deficiencies, such as a Hill Country education. And in this respect, the student Johnson was hardly alone at Southwest Texas State. What matters, of course, is where you end up, not where you started, but if Johnson was a lackluster student, he nevertheless acquitted himself remarkably well in other ways. His work in President Evans's office was exemplary, and what he learned there served him well later; it was certainly a step up from road construction. Johnson also distinguished himself as a debater and successfully involved himself in campus politics, actively siding with one student faction, the non-athletes, or White Stars, against another, the athletes, or Black Stars. Caro has argued that Johnson instigated the struggle for no other good reason than to quench, however momentarily, a seemingly unquenchable thirst for power and domination over others. It could also be that once committed to the contest, Johnson wanted to win, a feeling distinctly more human than monstrous. If he was overzealous and hurt others in the process, he was also young. In any event, his faction won, and the White Stars filled the elected offices and got to decide how to distribute student fees. But the experience that really stands out during Johnson's college years was his acceptance, out of financial necessity, during what would have been his junior year (1928–1929), of the job of principal and teacher at the Mexican-only school in Cotulla (population three thousand). While away, he nevertheless continued to earn college credits by taking correspondence courses.

Johnson's school, a two-year-old red brick building, brought Johnson face-to-face with the dark side of Texas's history and with his own Anglo male privilege. Deeply affected by the poverty of his students and their lack of any real opportunities, Johnson paternalistically responded by redoubling efforts to dehispanicize them. He insisted on an English-only policy and taught them Texas history as he had learned it, an iconic, one-sided, Anglo-centric vision of the state's past. The artist Henry McArdle captured this triumphalist story as well as anyone in the painting *Dawn at the Alamo* (1905). Johnson's own father, as a lawmaker, had played no small role in preserving the subject of this painting, the famous San Antonio mission-turned-fort, as a shrine to Texas nationalism. McArdle's historical canvas, which enjoys an honored place in the state capitol in Austin, left no doubt which side of the Texas Revolution God and history were on, an effect the Irish-born McArdle achieved in part through lighting and in part through cruel, even vicious caricatures of Mexican soldiers.

But if Johnson as a principal and schoolteacher in Cotulla had come face-to-face with Texas's history of conquest and colonialism, it was not the antebellum version of these things. As David Montejano has pointed out in *Anglos and Mexicans in the Making of Texas, 1836–1986* (1987), the history of Mexican-Anglo relations in South Texas had undergone a series of profound changes, the most recent of which — the collapse of the old ranch and family farming society, and its replacement with a thoroughly commercialized agriculture and migratory labor force — largely took place during Johnson's brief, at this point, lifetime. One of the most striking features of the social order during the first part of the twentieth century was its legal separation into Anglo and Mexican communities (as well as African American communities in African American–populated areas). In Cotulla, this division followed the Missouri-Pacific Railroad, with Anglos on the west side, and Mexicans on the "wrong" side of the tracks. In 1902, Seguin, a town located south of San Marcos, had the dubious distinction of being the first to establish a segregated Mexican school (which was arguably better, as Howard Rabinowitz has pointed out, than no school at all). By the time Johnson took over as principal of Welhausen in 1928, nearly 90 percent of the schools in South Texas had been segregated. Johnson may have been removed from this social malformation by virtue of growing up in the relatively remote and racially homogenous Hill Country. In more ways than one, he really was a product of an older Texas. His first administrative and teaching experience, however, introduced him to the new Texas and brought him directly in charge of a Jim Crow school.

Lyndon B. Johnson with his fifth, sixth, and seventh grade classes at Welhausen School, 1928. (LBJ Library, Pre Pres Collection)

Even so, Johnson refused to accept the separate and unequal reality behind the 1896 Supreme Court ruling *Plessy v. Ferguson*, whether or not he thought about the matter in precisely these terms. From the start, he insisted that the school board provide his charges with sporting equipment and made arrangements for Welhausen to play other, Anglo school teams. And he demanded that the other five Welhausen teachers (wives of Cotulla's more notable Anglo men) take their jobs as seriously as he did. When they balked, he threatened, with school board backing, to replace them with teachers from San Marcos. The Welhausen faculty soon gave in, allowing Johnson to run the school his way. By any account, this was a remarkable performance and experience for a twenty-year-old college junior. Moreover, there is no question that he left Welhausen better administered than it had been when he arrived.

Johnson returned to his studies at Southwest Texas State, which would take another year to finish. During that time, the country experienced the stock market crash of 1929, which marked the beginning of the Great Depression of the 1930s. This was hardly an auspicious time for Johnson or anyone to graduate and find gainful employment. Still, Johnson had favorably impressed virtually everyone with whom he had come into contact and was offered a job as a teacher and vice principal in another small town — Pearsall, Texas, which was located south of San Antonio, down the same road as Cotulla. He had dated a woman from Pearsall, Carol Davis, whom he had met in college. During his visits to the town, he came to know who was who, including the school superintendent. Johnson understood early the value of such contacts. But within weeks, he was offered a much better job teaching public speaking in Houston at Sam Houston High School. His uncle George, on his father's side, taught history there and helped Johnson get the job. He also put Johnson up. So just like that, soon after leaving college, Johnson had made it in the teaching profession.

As at Welhausen, Johnson gave Sam Houston High everything he had. He worked tirelessly and took the male debating team all the way to the state finals but lost on a split decision. And just as he had impressed everyone in Cotulla, Johnson quickly made a reputation for himself in Houston, which not only got him another contract but a raise as well. Johnson was clearly coming into his own. Indeed, he would one day become all but a force of nature — a great Texas tornado twisting across the nation's political landscape. He was not a full-blown weather event yet, certainly. He was not even a politician. By this time, however, one can already begin to see in the young Houston teacher a gathering storm, hear the wind start to twist and turn, and feel — sometimes intermittently, sometimes mercilessly — the sting of falling hail. And if you look hard enough at the meteorological Johnson, you might even catch a glimpse of a funnel-shaped cloud, still only partially formed, to be sure, and not yet dangerous, but an unpredictable phenomenon nonetheless. And, as it turned out, by November of the following academic year, Johnson would suddenly change careers from education to politics, moving every bit as forcefully as before, but now in an entirely new and different direction.

CHAPTER 2

Going National

JOHNSON'S interest in politics began long before his decision to accept Congressman Richard M. Kleberg's offer to serve as administrative assistant in his Washington office. It started at least as early as his boyhood trips to the state capital with his father, Sam. Politics was, after all, a family concern, and long a subject of conversation around the kitchen table. But more recently, and more significantly, in the summer of 1930, when Johnson was finishing college, he somehow found time to help run Welly Hopkins's state senate campaign. Hopkins, who was a friend of Johnson's father, was so impressed with Johnson's abilities that when he had the chance to return the favor, he went out of his way to help get the newly elected Kleberg to offer the twenty-one-year-old Johnson a job. On hearing about the idea, Johnson was "so excited he did not know what to say." He accepted the offer but prudently asked for, and was granted, a leave of absence from Sam Houston High—just in case things did not work out in Washington.

The sudden death of Harry McCleary Wurzbach, a Republican congressman, on November 6, 1931, vacated the seat for Texas's Fourteenth Congressional District. The district consisted of eleven counties in south-central Texas, much of it rich, cotton-producing land, and two urban centers: Corpus Christi, a port city on the gulf, and San Antonio, the home of the Alamo. A special election was scheduled for November 24. Dick Kleberg, a Democrat, ran against seven other candidates. He championed the platitudes of the day: states rights, local self-government, and all the "Old-Time Principles" of his party. After a short campaign, Kleberg went on to win (with Sam

Johnson's help, incidentally, in Blanco County) a plurality of more than five thousand votes. There was a year remaining on Wurzbach's two-year term, so Kleberg would have to run again the very next year. And this is where Johnson's prodigious energy and talent would serve. From the standpoint of excitement, there was no comparison between teaching and politics, but there was a difference in job security, risks Johnson was only too aware of based on his own family's experiences. He went to Washington anyway.

Richard Kleberg's personal situation, on the other hand, could not have been more different from Johnson's, a point that could hardly have been lost on the young schoolteacher. Richard Mifflin Kleberg, Sr., was born in 1887 on the King Ranch (after the cattle baron Richard King, who was at that time the richest man in Texas), located in Texas's coastal region between the Nueces River and the Rio Grande. The ranch was as large as it was famous. At 825,000 acres (or 1,300 square miles), it was actually bigger than the state of Rhode Island — a fact that Texas schoolchildren were once required to memorize. Johnson, who was ever prone to exaggeration, liked to say the ranch was bigger than Connecticut. Founded in 1853, not long after the war with Mexico, this enterprise got its start raising longhorns (later the ranch produced the famous Santa Gertrudis breed). The longhorns were brought up from south of the border, along with, evidently, the inhabitants of an entire Mexican village — imported laborers who were subsequently known as Los Kineños (the King's men). The ranch's storied and semifeudal history has served as shorthand for Texas history itself, as instanced in the critically acclaimed and popular film *Giant* (1956). Drawn from Edna Ferber's novel, this celluloid success depicted the epic story of the Benedicts, a fictional family (Rock Hudson played the likable patriarch), but one based on the very real King-Kleberg clan.

To put it another way, Dick Kleberg was hardly another poseur with more hat than cattle. He owned entire herds of them. Kleberg was part owner of the King Ranch and, along with his younger and more capable brother Robert J. Kleberg,

Jr., personally helped run its operations. (In 1947, Bob, who was president of the ranch, would get his picture on the cover of *Time* magazine, a fact that Texas writer Don Graham notes was the "only time a real rancher, rather than a politician posing as one, has achieved that status.") Indeed, according to the official historian of the King Ranch, Tom Lea, Dick Kleberg could rope and tie a breakaway calf in sixteen seconds: "no purse winner, but clearly a Congressional Record." In recognition of his impressive saddle skills, the press called Kleberg the Cowboy Congressman. Kleberg could drink whiskey, play poker and golf, and tell stories with the best of them. He also knew how to strut. In fact, he drove around Washington, to quote Don Graham, in a "customized King Ranch hunting car with its cutaway doors, running boards, rifle scabbards, and, most important, beverage holders." This was politically potent stuff, and it played well with the voters back home — a point of style, Texas style, not lost on a still very impressionable Johnson. Kleberg was elected six more times before being defeated in 1944 in the Democratic primary by Corpus Christi's John E. Lyle.

Kleberg was initially a New Deal supporter and, as member of the House Committee on Agriculture, worked on legislation of benefit to the farmer and rancher, namely, the bill establishing the Farm Credit Administration. And as a gentleman rancher and outdoorsman, he helped write the Migratory Bird Conservation Act and the Duck Stamp Law. After 1938, however, Kleberg increasingly began to distance himself from Roosevelt's liberal agenda. He was, in fact, one of many conservative Democrats to assert that the Democratic Party had left him, rather than the other way around. At the same time, the fortunes of the King Ranch were dramatically reversed during the thirties. The cattle ranch was, as nature would have it, seated above a subterranean sea of oil — a gift of geology that would put the ranch's books deep in the black and eventually turn the Texas operation into a global concern. Johnson went to work, then, not just for another freshman congressman, but for a man who all but exemplified Texas's romantic past as well as its future.

Moreover, 1932 — one of the few truly pivotal years in American political history—was the very year Johnson went to Washington to work for the Cowboy Congressman. Since the great crash on Wall Street four years before, the world economy had shrunk, amazingly and terrifyingly, to a third of its former size. The responses to this contraction would be felt for decades and, more immediately, would set the stage for dramatic political change at home and political extremism abroad. To more than one observer, capitalism's collapse seemed imminent. President Herbert Hoover's faith in economic liberalism, however, was unstinting, the great success of social democratic reforms notwithstanding, and remained undimmed to his dying day in 1964, three decades later—the same year that Arizona Republican Barry Goldwater would angrily take up the old faith that free markets alone create free men, in his campaign against Johnson for the U.S. presidency.

Hoover's positions on government and the economy reflected the values of an older, simpler, self-reliant America. They are worth taking a moment to consider, for while they served as the nation's default political philosophy, they provided the backdrop for the brilliant arc of American liberalism, from Roosevelt's New Deal to Johnson's Great Society, as the country experimented with strong government and an activist state. This said, Hoover—a mining engineer, self-made millionaire, and proud product of the American West (he was born in Iowa but grew up in Oregon)—was anything but an unthinking holdover from the nineteenth century. On the contrary, he was a highly intelligent and capable man, if a shockingly inept politician, despite having been elected to the highest office in the land. He clearly articulated his political philosophy in a speech he delivered during the 1928 presidential campaign. For Hoover, the greatest threat to the United States in recent times had been the wartime mobilization of the country to defeat imperial Germany. As Hoover put it:

During [World War I] we necessarily turned to the government to solve every difficult economic problem. The government having absorbed every energy of our people for war, there was no other solution. For the preservation of the state, the Federal Government became a centralized despotism which undertook unprecedented responsibilities, assumed autocratic powers, and took over the business of citizens. To a large degree, we regimented our whole people temporarily into a socialistic state. However justified in wartime, if continued in peacetime it would destroy not only our American system but with it our progress and freedom as well.

Hoover went on to frame the recent postwar past and to explain the policies of the last two postwar Republican administrations as well as lay out the fundamental principles that would guide his own, should he be elected:

When the war closed, the most vital of issues both in our own country and around the world was whether government should continue their wartime ownership and operation of many instrumentalities of production and distribution. We were challenged with a peacetime choice between the American system of rugged individualism and a European philosophy of diametrically opposed doctrines of paternalism and state socialism. The acceptance of these ideas would have meant the destruction of self-government through centralization of government. It would have meant the undermining of the individual initiative and enterprise through which our people have grown to unparalleled greatness.

Hoover's "rugged individualism" would be put to the test with the coming of the Great Depression, and for three years he saw to it that the American system, as he understood it, was given every opportunity for success. He stoutly resisted all calls for government action by insisting that "Prosperity [was] just around the corner." For the duration of his presidency, Hoover had things entirely his way, which was to leave in place the laissez-faire policies that had worked well enough for over a century. In Hoover's view, government involvement in the economy, apart from certain very limited, narrowly defined, and probusiness measures and expedients, was justified only in time of war. In his scheme of things, however, he did allow for public works projects — Boulder Dam, St. Lawrence Seaway. And with the paralysis of the private sector, he did back the idea of government loans to banks, railroads, corporations, and insurance companies through the federal agency of the Reconstruction Finance Corporation, charted in 1932. Hoover's principled positions and strongly held beliefs, while admirable, did nothing to stop the continued deepening of the economic crisis. The depression under his stewardship — or, as he would have it, non-stewardship — steadily worsened, turning into the Great Depression, or slump. The old ways Hoover championed had been tried and tried fully, to be sure, but in the end, the free market had failed, and spectacularly so. The world, in short, no longer worked the way America's business elite, informed by classical economics, thought it should.

Hoover would run again, offering the country more of the same — a less than inspiring prospect, especially for the 11 million Americans out of work. Not surprisingly, the worsening crisis had made Hoover very unpopular, and he even found himself personally blamed for the worldwide slump. His name became synonymous with unemployment. The Republicans were not optimistic about their chances in 1932. But despite how serious the nation's economic problems were, the American electorate was nevertheless in no mood for radical programs or third-party alternatives. Norman Thomas, for instance, the Socialist candidate, garnered fewer than a million votes; William Z. Foster, the Communist candidate, received a little over one hundred thousand votes. And there simply were no right-wing or fascist parties in contention. Instead, the American electorate overwhelmingly turned to the established alternative to the Republican Party: the Democrats. At the top of Democratic ticket was Franklin D. Roosevelt, the irrepressible and popular reform governor from the Empire State. Roosevelt's running mate was John Nance "Cactus Jack" Garner, the Speaker of the U.S. House of Representatives and congressman from Texas's Fifteenth Congressional District (Garner had been first elected to Congress back in 1902).

When Dick Kleberg asked his father, the seventy-eight-year-old Robert Justus Kleberg, for advice about running for Congress, R. J. exclaimed, "You're not going to run against John Garner!" believing that his son lived in Garner's district, which contained the King Ranch. When R. J. was reminded that his son actually resided in Nueces County, which lay outside Cactus Jack's old bailiwick, the old man responded, "Then run like hell." Dick Kleberg did, and won not only the special election, but with Johnson's help, the regular election in 1932 as well, when the Democrats easily took control of both Houses of Congress, signaling a major political realignment and giving Roosevelt a clear mandate for his New Deal for the American people. With redistricting in 1934, however, most of the King Ranch fell conveniently within the newly drawn boundaries of Kleberg's Fourteenth District, but in the new districting plan, the Fourteenth lost Bexar County and with it, San Antonio.

Like the Republicans, the Democrats, including the Texans John Garner, Dick Kleberg, and Kleberg's young, unbelievably hard-working secretary, Lyndon Johnson, also took the world war as the starting point for framing the recent political past. The war, in short, defined how an entire generation, "lost" or otherwise, saw things. For it was the defining national event, just as the Civil War had been before, and the Second World War would one day become. Whereas Hoover and the Republicans saw the war as a time in which the federal government became — if out of necessity — a "centralized despotism," it was the Harding, Coolidge, and Hoover' administrations that had fought to preserve the American system in the postwar era from "the doctrines of paternalism and state socialism." The Democrats, in contrast, as they had clearly stipulated in their 1932 party platform, saw the period since the war as marked by a series of disastrous policies: "economic isolation, fostering the merger of competitive businesses into monopolies and encouraging the indefensible expansion and contraction of credit for private profit at the expense of the public." For the Democrats, the war was not a necessary evil that had risked the nation's liberty, but an unrealized crusade — a failure they angrily decried:

Those who were responsible for these policies have abandoned the ideals on which the war was won and thrown away the fruits of victory, thus rejecting the greatest opportunity in history to bring peace, prosperity, and happiness to our people and to the world. They have ruined our foreign trade; destroyed the values of our commodities and products, crippled our banking system, robbed millions of our people of their life savings, and thrown millions more out of work, produced wide-spread poverty and brought the government to a state of financial distress unprecedented in time of peace. The only hope for improving present conditions, restoring employment, affording permanent relief to the people, and bringing the nation back to the proud position of domestic happiness and of financial, industrial, agricultural and commercial leadership in the world lies in a drastic change in economic governmental policies.

As Franklin Roosevelt's vice president, John Garner was front and center of the efforts to pass New Deal legislation — early on, anyway. Even before Kleberg, Garner, who was essentially a conservative Democrat, would break with Roosevelt's New Deal and start "sticking his knife in the president's back," as Harold Ickes, the secretary of the Interior, would put it. To Garner, some of Roosevelt's programs were just "plain damn foolishness." But early on, Cactus Jack's vast legislative knowhow and long experience on Capitol Hill proved indispensable to Roosevelt. Garner's prominence in Washington also marked a new and increasingly important role Texas would henceforth play in national politics. Kleberg confined himself largely to agriculture issues as well as golf and other pleasant diversions, while leaving the tending of constituents' matters, the more mundane and pedestrian, if absolutely vital, business of a congressman, entirely up to Johnson. And Kleberg's trust in his secretary was well placed indeed.

Johnson, who had taken up residence in a cubicle in the basement of the Grace Dodge Hotel, worked tirelessly for Kleberg. Lonely and homesick, he filled the voids in his life with work. He did have help, however, and from home. He hired two of his former students from Sam Houston High School, Gene Latimer and Luther (L.E.) Jones. They were glad to have job offers in the midst of the Great Depression. Johnson drove the two young men exceptionally hard, but never harder than he was prepared to work. The main job at hand was casework —the reading and responding to constituent mail, a lettered tide that came in daily. As the Great Depression worsened, the tide rose ever higher, threatening to drown the occupants in Room 258 in the old House Office Building. But Johnson heroically embraced this Sisyphusian labor and, in the process, learned exactly what was of concern to voters. And to respond (and respond) effectively to their numerous, relentless, and often urgent requests for help from the federal government, he had to learn how things in Washington really worked —a practical education for which there was no substitute. Moreover, he worked diligently to see to it that Kleberg's South Texas constituents took advantage of agricultural reform, such as the Agricultural Adjustment Administration, which addressed the key problem of overproduction by encouraging diversification. There were also other federal loans and subsidies made available through the Federal Land Bank and the Commodity Credit Corporation. All of this Johnson did —and more —and in so doing became the congressional secretary par excellence. The historian Paul Conkin goes further to suggest that Johnson actually "became the congressman from the Fourteenth District." And he is right.

This early experience in public service was formative and informed Johnson's subsequent political philosophy. Indeed, it would be hard to see how it would not have, given what the country was up against in those grim years. He knew that many of his constituents were desperate, that they were losing or had already lost everything, and that the only thing that stood between many of them and financial disaster was the hope that by acting collectively through the agency of the federal government they would get a better result than if they acted alone. It was basically the old idea that that there is strength in numbers. The Klebergs, Hoovers, and other beneficiaries of the "Old

Deal" would be all right, of course—most of them, anyway; their property was largely secure. Laws crafted long ago had made them rich, laws that had made a King Ranch possible in the first place. But by 1929, decades of accumulation by a few had resulted in an inverted and unstable pyramid of wealth, which finally tipped over. This disaster forced the "lords of yesterday" to accommodate themselves to sweeping reform, if very reluctantly. Kleberg, for instance, was deeply suspicious of the New Deal, which struck him as patently socialistic. And from his highly privileged perspective, it most certainly was. He would ultimately part company with Roosevelt's reforms, as would other conservative Democrats. But for a time, Johnson, with his Populist predilections and Hill Country common sense, convinced his boss to support Roosevelt, because the New Deal, whatever else it might have been, was popular.

While constituent service consumed a great deal of Johnson's time during Kleberg's first two fully elected terms, which coincided with Roosevelt's first term in the White House, it did not consume all of it, as was clear from his prominent role in the resuscitation of the Little Congress, a little league legislature made up of congressional workers. It was founded after the Great War but had lapsed into obscurity. Johnson saw an opportunity, however, in rousing the society from its sleep. In 1933, he engineered his election as speaker of the Little Congress and soon turned the body into an important debating society, since he intended debates there to prefigure the ones that counted on Capitol Hill. And the following year he attended Georgetown Law School, despite his California experience. His legal studies were short-lived, however, not because of time but because of interest. The law may have been the road most traveled to a career in politics, but it would not be Johnson's. Teaching was how he got his start in public life. But what did capture Johnson's full attention that same year was Claudia Alta "Lady Bird" Taylor, the daughter of Thomas Jefferson Taylor II, a wealthy Texas merchant and landowner who lived in the small town of Karnack in Harrison County, near the Louisiana border. Taylor had more of a southern than a western air

A young Claudia "Lady Bird" Taylor seated on a large rock. (LBJ Library, TFC Collection)

about him. Lady Bird grew up in this small-town, cotton-field, and bayou part of Texas. She graduated in 1933 with a bachelor of arts degree in journalism from the University of Texas and met Johnson in Austin on one of his trips home. Johnson courted her as if his life depended on it, which is how he approached much of life. This romance was threatened, however, by his having to return to Washington. Johnson put early-twentieth-century communication technologies to the test, and after two months Lady Bird finally said yes to his proposal of marriage. After a whirlwind engagement, the two were wed in San Antonio on November 17, 1934. After staying in the Plaza Hotel, the two went to Mexico for their honeymoon. Kleberg's secretary had married well — and everyone knew it.

Married now and having gone as far as he could go in Kleberg's congressional office, and further than any of his peers would have imagined possible, Johnson was ready for new chal-

lenges. During his tenure as secretary, he had come to the attention of the most powerful men in Washington and virtually all
the men in the Texas delegation — from Maury Maverick on the
left to Martin Dies on the right — including Congressman Sam
Rayburn, a powerful member of the House Committee on
Interstate and Foreign Commerce and a New Deal backer. Rayburn came from Bonham — a small town east of Sherman and
not far from the Red River — and also got his start teaching
school (but would go on and finish law school at the University
of Texas). Johnson (and Lady Bird) would become very close to
Rayburn, as Johnson had become close to other powerful men
in his life. Significantly, in 1937 Rayburn would become House
majority leader. Texas was indeed on its way to becoming a
political powerhouse — a twentieth-century development that
goes far in explaining Johnson's own impressive rise to power.

But Johnson was helping others on their way up as well. He
helped Maury Maverick of San Antonio, whose great-grandfather Samuel had refused to brand his cattle. Subsequently, all
unbranded cattle were called Maverick. Samuel, like Johnson's
ancestor John Wheeler Bunton, had signed the Texas Declaration of Independence. Johnson helped Maverick win the Democratic primary. Maverick, a decorated war hero (Silver Star),
who had fought and bled in the Argonne offensive, went on to
Congress. Interestingly, Maverick's politics were as left wing as
Kleberg's were right.

And Roosevelt would need Maverick, and many other likeminded lawmakers, to pass his Second New Deal, a more ambitious social reform agenda designed to benefit the common
man. In no way, however, did the New Deal — the first or the
second — ever challenge the basic premises of the old capitalist
older. The federal government's intervention in the economy to
help working people was, perhaps, no more radical than the
previous century's Congress opening up the American West
and distributing vast tracts of the public domain — worth billions in today's dollars — to homesteaders and corporations.
Once upon a time there was something in the nation's future
for everyone. But the massive economic and political inequali-

ties that followed these great nineteenth-century giveaways of land and natural resources undermined the very frontier egalitarianism that premised the government's disposition of the country's natural capital in the first place. This change ushered in the great American paradox.

The New Deal was, in a sense, about recreating a frontierlike egalitarianism or a fresh start for individuals and groups that had been left or shut out of earlier periods of prosperity. To do so was not only a revolutionary undertaking but an extremely difficult one, since it meant creating a state powerful enough to provide opportunity to millions of ordinary Americans in an economy that had been grossly mismanaged by the old guard. Thus, in 1935 the Social Security Act was passed into law, which addressed, among other things, the ancient fear of growing old and poor. By guaranteeing a minimum income to the nation's elderly, Social Security relieved a major source of anxiety, and with it, a major source of control employers could exercise over the lives of workers, especially the lives of older workers. Complementing this measure and passed the same year were the prolabor Wagner Act and the Wealth Tax Act, the latter a remarkably blatant, forthright, and long-overdue antiplutocratic measure intended, in the president's words, to prevent the "unjust concentration of wealth and economic power." Roosevelt went on to explain his progressive views more fully in his "June 19 Message to Congress on Tax Revision":

> Wealth in the modern world does not come merely from individual effort; it results from a combination of individual effort and of the manifold uses to which the community puts that effort. The individual does not create the product of his industry with his own hands; he utilizes the many processes and forces of mass production to meet the demands of a national and international market.
>
> Therefore, in spite of the great importance in our national life of the efforts and ingenuity of unusual individuals, the people in the mass have inevitably helped to make large fortunes possible. Without mass cooperation great accumulations of wealth would be impossible save by unhealthy speculation.

... Whether it be wealth achieved through the cooperation of the entire community or riches gained by speculation — in either case the ownership of such wealth or riches represents a great public interest and a great ability to pay.

And just as supply and demand should be subject to the discipline of the marketplace, for which there is no substitute, FDR believed government revenue and expenditures should, in the end, be brought into a state of equilibrium: "Because of the basis on which this proposed tax is to be levied and also because of the very sound public policy of encouraging a wider distribution of wealth, I strongly urge that the proceeds of this tax should be specifically segregated and applied, as they accrue, to the reduction of the national debt. By doing so, we shall progressively lighten the tax burden of the average taxpayer, and, incidentally, assist in our approach to a balanced budget."

Thus, the New Deal was not only about reform but fundamentally about shifting the balance of power within a postfrontier society to provide the basis for a real social democracy. As U.S. Supreme Court justice Louis Brandeis declared, "We can either have democracy in this country or we can have great wealth concentrated in the hands of few. But we can't have both." Little wonder the New Deal produced in the American Right such a deep and lasting opposition. In addition to the reforms mentioned above, Roosevelt signed legislation in April 1935 establishing the Works Progress Administration, headed up by Roosevelt's righthand man, Harry Hopkins, and at Eleanor Roosevelt's urging, Roosevelt issued an executive order creating the National Youth Administration (NYA).

The failure of the private sector to create employment was hurting the nation's youth. As one of Harry Hopkins's aides put it, "The young are rotting without jobs and there are no jobs." Eleanor Roosevelt had long been concerned with the "plight of the country's youth" but knew that Hopkins and Aubrey Williams of Alabama, Hopkins's deputy administrator (who would be in charge of the NYA), were reluctant to bring up the issue to the president because, according to the first lady,

"They felt a great many people who were worried by the fact that Germany had regimented its youth might feel we were trying to do the same thing in this country and they might not look upon the move with favor." Eleanor Roosevelt persuaded her husband to create the NYA anyway, quoting the president as saying, "If it is the right thing to do for the young people, then it should be done. I guess we can stand the criticism." He also knew his young countrymen and women and doubted "if our youth can be regimented in this way or in any other way."

With the creation of the NYA, Aubrey Williams would need state directors. Given Johnson's demonstrated ability and knowledge of government, his political loyalty, his enthusiastic and unqualified support of the New Deal, Johnson, although only twenty-six years old at the time, seemed a perfect fit for the job. At least Sam Rayburn thought so, and his opinion in matters of patronage mattered. Remarkably, Maury Maverick and Martin Dies thought so, too. It was all worked out, and quickly, with Johnson eagerly accepting Aubrey's appointment on July 25. He was anxious, of course, to get out of Kleberg's shadow and dedicate himself to, and take full responsibility (and receive all the credit) for, something big and important, in this case the improvement of the poor youth of Texas by either keeping them in school and college or providing them with practical skills and useful work. This was a job for which Johnson felt a strong affinity. It was also a job that was made to order for anyone with political ambition, which Johnson possessed in full measure. He had good reason to want to work every county and political unit in Texas. But more than that, the appeal of the work said something larger about the New Deal itself, for the reform program drew into public life many of the country's most able and talented men and women. In this regard, Johnson was but one of many. His work at the NYA, however, was exemplary. In fact, under his direction, the Texas agency became a model for the rest of the country, and although the NYA helped blacks as well as whites, in Texas and elsewhere, Johnson shrewdly drew as little attention to that fact as was practicable, thus avoiding any white backlash. He understood well the implacable hostility of whites to the idea of government helping Americans of African descent. As for the public works projects, such as the popular roadside rest areas, the NYA, the Civilian Conservation Corps, and other New Deal agencies met what was clearly an enormous need, fulfilling a backlog of work orders for thousands of projects and repairs, from hiking trails to city sidewalks, providing money, resources, and labor that contributed much to nearly everyone's quality of life.

The South and the West benefited the most from these programs because they were the country's least developed regions. The South's backwardness was, of course, largely self-inflicted. The failure to create an independent slave republic in the previous century had economically devastated the region. The abolition of black slavery (there was no white involuntary servitude) was a result that at least gave the great slaughter a purpose and justification, which it would not otherwise have possessed, as Lincoln noted in his second inaugural address. Predictably, the South did not see it that way. And in the war's aftermath, the region's white elites seemed determined to weaken the South even further by creating two communities segregated along strict racial lines. The vision was clarity itself: impose a one-party dictatorship over a two-race South — or, in the words of the day, establish a "white supremacy" in the region.

The subordination and bifurcation of an affluent society would have been expensive enough. To have willingly divided a poor, defeated society, which depended on selling cotton in a glutted world market for income, ensured that the dream of a New South — one that was increasingly industrial and economically diversified — went unrealized. The South's rejection of Radical Reconstruction, an exogenous experiment, after all, to create a multiracial democracy, doomed the region to a long period of social retardation instead of general progress for the South's white, black, and (in Texas) Hispanic communities. The weaker and poorer black community was affected by segregation far more so than the numerically larger white community, the latter of which jealously and violently (through lynching, intimidation, and any other means necessary) retained control of what was left of the region's major assets, resources, and decision-making processes. The ugly and stunted results of these endogenous public policies, which in effect marked a low-grade continuation of the Civil War, were long hidden from view behind sweet-smelling magnolias, sprawling oaks, and hanging Spanish moss; but they were at last exposed for the entire world to see by the uprooting winds of the Great Depression, which hit the South like a hurricane. In response, President Roosevelt declared in 1938 that the South was the nation's "number 1 economic problem," tactfully leaving aside explanations of its cause. Still, for some southerners, such as U.S. senator John Elvis Miller from Arkansas, Roosevelt's attention raised from the dead the specter of another Reconstruction. What Miller wanted was for the North to leave the South alone.

The American West, in contrast to the American South — with the notable exception of Texas, which is as much a part of the South as it is a part of the West, owed its underdevelopment to a classic colonial relationship. In short, the western economy was based largely on the export of raw materials to the industrialized northeast, namely minerals, cattle and livestock, lumber, and petroleum. Unlike the South, the West's agriculture was only a minor part of its overall economy, even if the environmental disaster of the Dust Bowl seemed to suggest otherwise. The Territory of Alaska offers an extreme case in point, although it was situated in the frigid North, America's "last frontier," rather than the arid West.

When in 1939 Ernest Gruening arrived in the last frontier as President Roosevelt's governor, Gruening found the territory totally in the thrall of corporate interests and outside capital, namely the mining and the canned salmon industry. Further, in 1920 the U.S. Congress had, in effect, granted Seattle's shipping industry a monopoly over the transportation of goods to Alaska. Angered at the territory's treatment by an axis of mercantilists in Washington and capitalists on Wall Street, the ardent New Dealer demanded to know "whether Alaska shall be built up for the people of Alaska in conformity with American principles and standards, or whether it shall continue to be governed for and by outside interests whose sole concern is to take out of Alaska as much as they can, as far as they can, and to leave as little as possible."

For many, this question was no less applicable to the land south of the forty-ninth parallel and west of the hundredth meridian, a region that writer, historian, and westerner turned East Coast intellectual Bernard DeVoto described in a 1934 article in *Harper's Magazine* as the "looted," "betrayed," "sold out," and "plundered" West. Against such historic and contemporary abuse, it was little wonder the West produced a representative figure who, DeVoto observed, was portrayed, or rather caricatured, in the cartoons as "Gaunt and wild-eyed," who "rides a whirlwind or rushes over a cliff, invariably dragging the republic with him." And "the lightning round his head" was "labeled Socialism, Bolshevist Daydreams, or National Bankruptcy." In short, the struggle to gain control over their own destiny is what pushed westerners over and over again to embrace programs of radical agrarianism. As DeVoto sharply put it, "Very early the West memorized a moral: the wealth of a county belongs to the owners, and the owners are not the residents or even the stockholders but the manipulators. Gold, silver, copper, all the minerals, oil — you need not look for their increase in the West, nor even among the generations of widows and orphans thoughtfully advised to invest in them by trust companies. The place to look for that increase is the trust companies, and the holding companies."

DeVoto was deeply influenced by Walter Prescott Webb's "fine book" *The Great Plains*, in which the author examined the nation's procrustean attempts to make laws that proved maladapted for the treeless, waterless, and horizontal environment that obtained in America's great grassy midsection. Webb followed up on his book, and on DeVoto's *Harper's* piece, with *Divided We Stand: The Crisis of a Frontierless Democracy* (published in 1937 and revised in 1944). The Texan thundered and threatened the imperial colonizing North from his ivory tower in Austin. This thesis turned the South and West into the long-standing victims of Yankee cupidity. The way out of this second "sectional crisis," Webb contended, was for the North "not to allow its corporate greed and blind self-interest to ruin a great nation," but instead to adopt a "Good Neighbor Policy at home," as it had toward Latin America. The Good Neighbor policy was an apt if ironic metaphor for a Texan to use, because it was formulated to soften America's imperial image in Latin America, where it had arrogantly intervened militarily for decades. This change in foreign policy was started under Hoover, but it was the Roosevelt administration that realized its full public relations value. When the United States acquiesced in Mexico's nationalization of its own oil industry in March 1938, which for the Latin republic was tantamount to a second declaration of independence, it suggested that the new U.S. policy was, in fact, more than just public diplomacy. In a sense, the New Deal was a Good Neighbor policy at home, even if it evidently did not go far enough for Webb. Other Texans — Richard Kleberg, John Nance Garner, Martin Dies — believed the New Deal had gone too far and concluded that the threat of statism to liberty had begun, by the end of the decade, to outweigh the threats of plutocracy and corporate control.

In 1944, in a revised edition of *Divided We Stand*, Webb changed his mind about the way "to get rid of sectionalism." Maybe he realized that in light of Texas's betrayal of, or violent secession from, Mexico in 1836, his call on the North to adopt a Good Neighbor policy might be too much for his readers to stomach. In any event, he now appealed to westerners, rather than Yankees, asking them to embrace the Democratic Party, thereby turning it into a truly national political party. Since Webb believed the Republican Party — the party of big business, the rich, sectional supremacy, and a failed economic order — would have little appeal to the southerner, only the Democrats had a chance of building a political base in all three sections. This second strategy was superior to the first one in that it was based on the self-interest of strangers rather than their kindness.

In 1937, however, far from expanding the party's base, Democrats found themselves struggling to keep hold of their conservative members. The turning point for many, of course, was Roosevelt's attempt that year to reorganize the judiciary, which he rightly deemed as hostile to the New Deal. The president's proposal to build a more sympathetic judiciary was bold. As he saw it, "Whenever a judge or justice of any federal court has reached the age of seventy and does not avail himself of the opportunity to retire on a pension, a new member shall be appointed by the president then in office, with the approval, as required by the Constitution, of the Senate of the United States."

Critics charged the president with trying to make himself a virtual dictator, but Roosevelt defended himself in a fireside chat to the nation:

> I want to talk with you very simply about the need for present action in this crisis. . . . [I have] described the American form of government as a three-horse team provided by the Constitution to the American people so that their field might be plowed. The three horses are, of course, the three branches of government — the Congress, the Executive, and the Courts. Two of the horses are pulling in unison today; the third is not. Those who have intimated that the president of the United States is trying to drive that team, overlook the simple fact that the President, as Chief Executive, is himself one of the three horses.

At the same time that Roosevelt was trying to get the third horse to pull with him, the openly socialistic and widely popular policies of Mexico's president, Lázaro Cárdenas, served to reconfirm the statist fears of many, including conservative Democrats in oil-rich Texas and elsewhere who saw Roosevelt as a charioteer cracking a whip rather than a farmer gently guiding a plow.

It was into this ideological cauldron that Johnson had plunged, but his astute political judgment (and his father's advice) served him well. As director of the NYA, he had made a name for himself in Texas, and he had even come to the favorable attention of Eleanor Roosevelt herself. When Representative James P. Buchanan of the Tenth Congressional District, which included Blanco County in the Hill Country, died on February 22, 1937, Johnson saw his opportunity. He resigned from the NYA forthwith and, after announcing his candidacy from the porch of his home in Johnson City, ran against nine other candidates. Governor James V. Allred, a New Dealer who knew, and not so quietly supported, Johnson, called a special election, to be decided by a plurality rather than a majority of votes, for April 10. The odds seemed very much against the twenty-eight-year-old Johnson. After all, his work for Kleberg and the Texas NYA did little to bring him to the attention of the average voter in the Tenth District, which included Austin but also much smaller and relatively isolated communities and rural areas.

But if Johnson had disadvantages, including a field of more experienced and better-known candidates, he also had the financial backing of his father-in-law as well as many other supporters. Indeed, Robert Caro estimates that Johnson's first campaign cost between $75,000 and $100,000, making it, he darkly notes, "one of the most expensive congressional races in Texas history up to that time." The implication is that Johnson was beholden to supporters, namely Alvin J. Wirtz. Wirtz was the moving force, legal genius, and behind-the-scenes operator of the Lower Colorado River Authority, a public agency instituted in 1934 by the Texas legislature but funded entirely through the sale of electricity, water, and other services. Caro does not explain, however, how Johnson's relationship with backers differed in kind, if perhaps in degree, from any other politician. Johnson had other valuable assets, of course: there was his boundless energy, his almost uncanny political ability and adroit use of local media, and the support and loyalty of his now many friends, going back to his college and Hill Country days. In short, Johnson did not win so much as overwhelm. But as important as all of these things were to his victory, there was also the simple and indisputable fact that the Tenth District was Roosevelt country, as was much of the nation for that matter. From the beginning of the campaign, Johnson set himself sharply apart as the Roosevelt candidate. Indeed, his slogan was "Roosevelt, Roosevelt, Roosevelt: One Hundred Percent for Roosevelt," and he let voters know his support for FDR included backing the controversial "court-packing" plan, a smart political decision because it turned what was otherwise an obscure Texas election into a national event—a point not lost on the president.

The voters sent Mr. Johnson to Washington, an FDR man and a New Dealer through and through. Today, Johnson is remembered as the careworn president, the most powerful man in the world who nevertheless found himself weighed down by war and civil strife. In 1937, however, he cut a very different figure. He was young and brilliant; he radiated purpose and exuded confidence; he very much looked like a man destined for greater things. He appealed to men and was attractive to women. Indeed, Johnson emanated his own force field, which drew in virtually everybody who came in contact with it; this force even attracted men with powerful magnetic pulls of their own, including the greatest U.S. politician of the twentieth century, FDR.

On May 11, 1937, the president met the newly elected congressman down in Galveston, Texas. Finishing up a fishing trip for tarpon in the Gulf of Mexico, FDR was on his way to College Station to inspect ROTC cadets at Texas Agricultural and Mining College (Texas A&M). Johnson rode on the train with the president, and at FDR's invitation, Johnson accompanied him on to Fort Worth, or Cowtown as natives called it because of the stockyards there and the city's association with the famous cattle drives of the 1870s. Fort Worth's commercial and more culturally sophisticated urban rival, Dallas, with which it shares the Trinity River basin, lay just to the east. What these two remarkable politicians said to each other as their train rolled north, and all day long at that, down those long and lonely Texas tracks is not recorded—those kind of truly historic conversations rarely are. But what is known is that as farm and field passed by—scenes of an older small-town and rural America—FDR looked to the future and saw in Johnson a man whom he could count on as a political ally and to whom he could offer help. Accordingly, the president steered Johnson to the House Committee on Naval Affairs, where Johnson could quietly but steadfastly serve the administration's interests, help his friends, and in turn gain a perspective of the world far beyond the landlocked Tenth District.

In Bernard DeVoto's "Plundered Province" piece in *Harper's*, he had referred to the eastern image of the westerner as one consisting of "the national wild man, the thunderer-bringer, disciple of madness, begetter of economic heresy, immortal nincompoop deluded by maniac visions, forever clamoring, forever threatening the nation's treasury, forever scuttling the ship of state." DeVoto might have added "isolationist" as well, given the strength of the western opposition to involvement in European affairs, as expressed by such political leaders as William E. Borah of Idaho, Burton K. Wheeler of Montana, Hiram Johnson of California, and Gerald P. Nye of North Dakota.

Senator Nye, a Republican and former newspaperman from Bismarck, had only the year before released the *Report of the Special Committee on Investigation of the Munitions Industry*. The Nye commission found, among other things, "that any close associations between munitions and supply companies on the one hand and the [military] service departments on the other hand, of the kind which existed in Germany before the world war, constitutes an unhealthy alliance in that it brings into being a self-interested political power which operates in the name of patriotism and satisfies interests which are, in large part, purely selfish, and that such associations are an inevitable part of militarism, and are to be avoided in peacetime at all costs." Such conclusions, which basically reaffirmed the country's deep-seated antimilitary tradition and ancient fears of standing armies, were accepted in the 1930s as a matter of course — U.S. Civics 101 — and led to the easy passage of the Neutrality Acts of 1935, 1936, and 1937. This legislation left President Roosevelt with the difficult political task of persuading the American people that the growing threats from abroad were a greater evil than the threat that an alliance between

industry and the military posed to liberty at home — that isolationism was a poor moral choice in a world engulfed by violence, from the bombing of Guernica in Spain, the carnage of
which the artist Picasso immortalized, to the "rape" of Nanking
in China.

Right from the beginning, Johnson distinguished himself
not only by his unequivocal support of Roosevelt and the New
Deal, especially in terms of reclamation, rural electrification,
and public housing, but also by strongly supporting military
preparedness. Johnson also championed efficiency and economy in government, old-fashioned values that took on new
meaning for New Dealers, especially Roosevelt. The Democratic Party's bold willingness to experiment in using government, public policy, and deficit spending to solve the nation's
economic and social problems was never divorced from an
equally keen sense of fiscal responsibility. If the New Deal was
America's Third Revolution, as some historians argue since it
profoundly changed the relationship between the federal government and the states, the New Deal shared one important
thing in common with the previous two revolutions, the Civil
War and the War of Independence; namely, they were all essentially conservative, fundamentally cautious exercises in the use
of power.

In the same magazine article in which DeVoto remarked on
the perception of the westerner as "wild man," he also observed
"a queer thing" about the westerner:

A mere change of clothes gives him a different meaning on
quite as large a scale. Put a big hat on his head, cover the
ragged overalls with hair pants and let high heels show beneath them, knot a bandana around his neck — and you have
immediately one of the few romantic symbols in American
life. He has ceased to be a radical nincompoop and is now a
free man living greatly, a rider into the sunset, enrapturer of
women in dim theaters, solace of routine-weary men who
seek relief in woodpulp, a figure of glamour in the reverie of
adolescents, the only American who has an art and a literature devoted wholly to his celebration.

As the secretary of the Cowboy Congressman, Johnson had seen firsthand this "queer thing," the curious potency of western symbolism. He did not have the money of Kleberg. Few did. But he was from Texas, and while he did not don hair leggings or knot a bandana around his neck, he did sport Stetsons, and he did relish playing up his western, as distinct from his southern, heritage for all it was politically worth. And in 1951, when he could finally afford it, he would acquire his own "King Ranch," if miniature in comparison, in the Pedernales Valley—and stock it with Herefords.

But the West was not an affectation only. It was also a place, a dry and dangerous place, but one that with the proper application of federal power had enormous potential, something Johnson fully and deeply grasped. But progress in the West depended on harnessing the region's hydraulic power, which in turn depended on creating a technical and political elite that had the knowledge and wherewithal to deliver and manage the western waters. The Oklahoma folksinger Woody Guthrie expressed the gist of the idea in song after visiting the Grand Coulee Dam on the Columbia River:

> Uncle Sam took up the challenge in the year of thirty three
> For the farmer and the factory and all of you and me
> He said, "Roll along, Columbia, you can roll down to the
>   sea,
> But river, while you're rambling, you can do some work for
>   me."

As congressman, Johnson worked closely with Wirtz's Lower Colorado River Authority. One of the authority's first projects to be completed was Hamilton Dam, renamed Buchanan Dam after Johnson's predecessor, James P. Buchanan, the chairman of the House Appropriations Committee, in recognition of Buchanan's work in securing federal funds for the project. Intended primarily for power generation rather than flood control, the dam, located northwest of Austin, was completed in time to mitigate the effects of one of the worst floods in the river's history, which occurred in July 1938. Johnson would have a much bigger hand in the construction of the Marshall Ford Dam, built downriver of Buchanan Dam in 1941 by the Brown brothers, Herman and George (of Brown & Root, Inc.), the Houston-based construction company with which Johnson would have a long, infamous, but mutually and extremely profitable relationship. It was the Marshall Ford that finally tamed the Texas Colorado River and brought Central Texas into the twentieth century—and turned Brown & Root into a construction giant.

At the dedication of Buchanan Dam, an interesting multiple-arch structure, which was held on October 16, 1937, it was Johnson's honor to introduce Harold Ickes, Roosevelt's powerful secretary of the Interior. Johnson's benedictory remarks on this occasion to his "Friends and Fellow-Texans" reveal in clear and compelling terms what he thought the New Deal meant to the West and to the rest of the country. The timbre and modulation of Johnson's voice as it carried over the dry and open Texas air can only be imagined, but here are his words:

> We have here the realizations of the visions of a great president, who finds in this project one unit in a vast national program to conserve America's natural resources and to turn waste to useful purpose. We see here a *living* unit of the comprehensive program he has worked out for the centuries to come, and laid the foundations for in his Seven-Regional-TVA [Tennessee Valley Authority] proposal. We see here the accomplishment of his dream to place idle men — men thrust out of the channels of work and livelihood by an antiquated economic system — on jobs which not only will support them, but will benefit them and theirs years to come.

From this sweeping vision of national purpose, Johnson went on to articulate in the same speech the significance of Buchanan Dam to the citizens of Burnet County and to the greater Hill Country that stretched southward:

> This dam is a monument to those who long have gazed upon the raging floods of spring and fall, racing down the Colorado Valley, tearing and destroying as they passed, uprooting

trees, caving in farms, ravaging crops, and sowing general destruction and desolation. It is a monument to those who have seen the uselessness in wasting those vast forces when they are needed so sorely to do work undone and yet to be done on every hand. It is a monument to those who believe that the power spent in those floods ought to operate farm machinery, light farm homes, pump water for irrigation, bring cheap and unlimited power and light to cities large and small, or help man along to greater enterprises for his own good.

Dams are as old as civilization, of course, and were probably as much appreciated in ancient Mesopotamia as they were in modern Texas. What was new, however, was that Buchanan Dam, followed by the Marshall Ford Dam (renamed the Mansfield Dam) and other projects, enabled Johnson — through the power and agency of the federal government — to effect the electrification of the Hill Country. The importance of this political accomplishment simply cannot be overestimated; it brought his Tenth District constituency out of the primitive conditions and hardships of the nineteenth-century rural frontier into the galvanized and wired twentieth, with its modern advantages and conveniences. Even the prosecutorial Robert Caro, the kind of man Oscar Wilde had in mind when the poet and playwright feared that biography had become but another of death's terrors, was reluctantly forced to admit that Johnson had succeeded in using his power to make life in the Hill Country materially and substantially better. Rural electrification was hardly unique to the Hill Country. In fact, it was but one of numerous New Deal programs designed to modernize the country. What stands out was Johnson's ability to master all levels of power — federal and local, public and private — to bring light back home, as if he were a latter-day Prometheus, except his act would not anger the gods but would inspire the loyalty of a grateful electorate.

The Hill Country, like its Ozark and Appalachia counterparts arching away far to the northeast, was marked by a stubborn

Congressman Lyndon B. Johnson and Mrs. Mattie Malone examine an electric light fixture, 1941. (LBJ Library, Austin Statesman Collection)

poverty and backwardness. As a congressman from Texas, Johnson could do little about the problems of the two mountainous regions that lay far outside his district, but the underdevelopment that existed at home was another matter entirely. It would be an exaggeration to assert that the nation's Sunbelt, a new and dynamic region spanning the southern-tiered states from Florida to Texas to California—the Old Spanish Borderlands—began with the dedication of Buchanan Dam. But it was not a matter of chance that Johnson's dramatic political ascent, starting with the dedication, coincided with the rise of the Sunbelt and the westward tilt the nation would experience in the ensuing postwar decades.

CHAPTER 3

The Sunbelt Also Rises

IT IS true that the Second World War ended the Great Depression. Or, to put it another way, the greatest military disaster in human history somehow had an upside: it brought the U.S. economy — which possessed plenty of excess capacity — out of a decade-long slump. It is also true that the New Deal helped forge a sense of national unity in the face of great economic hardship, a unity that enabled the United States to fight and win the war. The two struggles were, of course, related in many ways. Perhaps most directly, Roosevelt's Four Freedoms ("freedom of speech and expression," "freedom of worship," "freedom from want," and "freedom from fear") were, in effect, a declaration of a New Deal creed for the entire world. Roosevelt, like Woodrow Wilson before him, tried to convert domestic reform and the strengthening of democracy into an international program. Both men were successful to a degree. Thus, in the face of the surprise attack on Pearl Harbor, Americans were willing to go fight *against* tyranny in Asia and Europe, but after years of reform and progress, they were also willing to fight *for* something — namely, their freedom and way of life at home, which under the leadership of Roosevelt had become a far more inclusive and economically just way of life than had been the case.

The prospect of real security for all instead of just a privileged few had brought about a profound and liberating change, which had the effect of turning Americans into formidable foes, remarkably united in purpose, and of turning the United States into the leader of the free world. Democracy is indeed a great cause and one for which people will make sacrifices — the ultimate, if necessary. In a sense, Roosevelt had turned Wilson on his head. Americans went off to fight in the North Atlantic and the Pacific less to make the world safe for democracy than for their own democracy—newly invigorated—in a dangerous world. Moreover, the struggle was not over with victory in Europe and Japan. Indeed, the urgency of the Second World War and the building of an international order around America's newly won place in the world would quickly give way to a seemingly endless and terribly costly cold war. The Soviet Union, America's wartime ally turned rival, possessed its own blueprints and competing architecture for the postwar world.

During the crucial era of depression and world war, Johnson remained closely identified with Roosevelt, the New Deal, and preparedness. He supported a new selective service system and opposed the "America Firsters" and "other pot-shotters at American democracy," criticizing one of their spokesmen, the famed aviator Charles A. Lindbergh, whose praises he had once sung as a college student. And he voted for such path-breaking legislation as the minimum wage bill, which erected a wage floor for the country, but nevertheless left the economic underpinnings of white supremacy in the South unchallenged by excluding farm and domestic labor from its provisions.

The limits of New Deal reform in the South were very real, of course. The post-Reconstruction social order survived largely intact. But the very improvement that whites in the old Confederacy and elsewhere experienced as a result of the government reforms and programs of the 1930s, when Americans realized the advantages of combining their resources on a national level, would indirectly help to undermine the practice of overt racial discrimination. As long as there was relatively little difference in the living standards of whites and blacks, the legal doctrine separate but equal could be maintained.

However, New Deal reform and the tremendous economic and social pressures created by the wartime economy threatened to expose, even as it widened, the country's old racial divide. This growing economic inequality was averted, at least in part, by the success of A. Philip Randolph, a prominent black labor leader. Randolph convinced President Roosevelt, who issued Executive Order 8802, prohibiting government contractors from engaging in employment discrimination, to ensure that black workers received a real share of the new defense industry jobs. This action allowed Roosevelt to keep U.S. production humming, without which there could be no "arsenal of democracy." And ever mindful of political realities, Roosevelt's decision also did little to upset the racial status quo or, and this was the main concern, the southern wing of the Democratic Party. It was not until after the war that the Jim Crow edifice would be dismantled, beginning in 1948 with President Harry S. Truman's order to desegregate the armed forces. As the war approached, Johnson adeptly staked out positions on foreign policy issues and navigated the economic and social changes of this transformative period.

Given Johnson's scrupulous attention to the needs of his constituents, his seat was secure, probably for as long as he wanted to serve in Congress. But he was far more ambitious than that. In 1941, with the sudden death of Senator Morris Sheppard on April 9, Johnson ran in a special election for the seat, losing very closely to Wilbert Lee "Pass the Biscuits, Pappy" O'Daniel, when a relative handful of amended votes from East Texas, suspiciously running in Pappy's favor, were reported too late for any kind of effective response by Johnson's campaign. Challenging the returns was out of the question given Johnson's own share of electioneering chicanery.

This setback for Johnson was not just a question of last-minute, albeit decisive, maneuvering, however. Pappy was a superb politician and a master of the bait-and-switch, although he is often dismissed as a rather humorous eccentric of Texas politics; indeed, he remains a durable caricature in American popular culture. Pappy had a large fan base due to his popular radio show (which aired on station KFJZ), in which he delighted Texas audiences with the western swing music performed by the fiddle band The Light Crust Doughboys. Pappy found that mixing music with old-fashioned homilies proved a very profitable way to promote the virtues of his Hillbilly Flour

Congressman Lyndon B. Johnson campaigning for the U.S. Senate, 1941. (LBJ Library, Austin Statesman Collection)

Company. It was also a good way to court the electorate, a lesson not lost on Johnson, just as the appeal of Kleberg's cowboy persona was not lost on him. Indeed, Johnson, flush with Brown & Root money and with Roosevelt's strong backing, had tried to out-radio, out-vaudeville, and outspend Pappy, but lost anyway, by 1,311 votes. Still, it was quite a show.

Prior to the senate race, Pappy, a well-to-do businessman, had already learned to pose as a simple hillbilly, run on the Ten Commandments (there is no record, incidentally, of an anti–Ten Commandments politician, party, or platform, either in Texas or the rest of the country), and identify himself with a moderate progressive agenda. This formula got Pappy elected governor in 1938. This public persona notwithstanding, Pappy was actually quite conservative. He was hostile to labor—a position he shared with many other Texas Democrats, including John Nance Garner. Indeed, Pappy tried to go after labor, now empowered by the Wagner Act, with an antistrike, antiviolence bill. Pappy was an old-fashioned capitalist and jealous of the prerogatives he enjoyed, so it is not surprising that he, like so many others in the Texas political establishment, worked hard against the democratization of economic decision making (after all, responsibilities and risks were not equally shared between management and labor), a feared outcome of a strong and effective labor movement. American industry and business may have initially been supportive of the New Deal, but those days were short-lived and long gone, and no more so than down in Texas. Reaction had calcified there but not among average voters, who continued to favor Roosevelt's domestic policies. (Indeed, in 1940, FDR was elected to an unprecedented third term; he would win yet again in 1944.) Less typical among politicians, however, was the hostility Pappy showed to academia and the principle of academic freedom, as evidenced in his appointments to the University of Texas Board of Regents. The American Association of University Professors responded accordingly and censored UT, an embarrassment the state endured for nine years. And Pappy was no less hostile to the press, which he tried to counter with his own news organ, *The W. Lee O'Daniel News*. In a dress rehearsal of McCarthyism, Pappy showed that it was far easier to attack vague internal communist threats, always more imagined than real, than to challenge popular New Deal measures directly.

Long before Senator Joseph McCarthy and other politicians discovered they could turn fear into votes, but not long after the creation of the House Committee on Un-American Activities (HUAC) was formed in 1938 and chaired by fellow Texan Martin Dies— Pappy claimed there was a "fifth column" in Texas. Pappy used this fear to get reelected as governor in 1940. Johnson knew Texas as well as anyone and in 1943 voted to continue HUAC, even though Dies believed that the New Deal was a communist conspiracy. It is curious, however, that the elected officials and representatives of Texas, a state so infamously disloyal and yet so proud of this checkered history— it was "un-Mexican" in 1835 and "Un-Union" in 1861—would so passionately support HUAC. Superpatriotism and ideological correctness were probably overcompensation at some level in the state's mass psyche for its perfidious and decidedly unpatriotic past—a phenomenon not unlike religious conversion of a notorious sinner into a self-righteous and intolerant boor. In fact, HUAC may be likened to a secular and modern equivalent to the old Spanish inquisition. Of course, there were real fascists and communists in the United States, just as there were real heretics in Spain.

In any event, the next year Pappy, a populist imposter, defeated Johnson, who was a bona fide New Dealer, for the U.S. Senate and went on to win reelection in 1942, this time defeating another New Dealer and former Texas governor, James V. Allred. In Austin, Coke Stevenson—an anti–New Deal Democrat—would succeed Pappy and go on to be a very popular governor. The state's politics were clearly shifting rightward.

By then, the Empire of Japan, which was already at war with a weakened and divided China, had launched another war in late 1941 and early 1942, this time against Great Britain and the United States, in a brazen bid to create a Greater East Asia Co-Prosperity Sphere, an act as reckless as Germany's earlier decision to invade the Soviet Union. Unlike the Japanese ideology of expansion, however, the Nazi's *Lebensraum* contained not even a hint of mutual benefit. The fascist challenge was perhaps at bottom an attack on globalization, a morally ambiguous process guided as if by an invisible hand, in which the world was being rapidly, sometimes violently, integrated into a single, if hardly harmonious, market and community. Globalization had been conceived long ago by the actions of fifteenth-century Portuguese mariners and later midwifed into being by nineteenth-century Atlantic-world imperialists. By the twentieth century, the United States, which owed its own origins to an earlier, mercantilist phase of globalization, had rapidly emerged to become its dominant and most loyal player, not out of an idealistic belief in one world, to be sure, but out of pure self-interest, a perhaps more reliable but far from infallible guide in foreign affairs. And the concurrent economic transformation of a world based on agriculture and trade to one devoted to commerce, industry, and technological innovation ushered in the modern era in which governments had to learn how to manage the happier problems of abundance rather than scarcity, business rather than Malthusian cycles. But globalization, with its contradictory mix of promises and problems, had been stalled by the worldwide Great Depression and now was imperiled by the autarchic, atavistic, ferociously nationalistic, relentlessly expansionistic, and qualifiedly modernistic forces that had recently sprung up like tall noxious weeds on a vacant lot, not only in Tokyo but in Rome and in Berlin.

With the news of the attack on U.S. naval forces at Pearl Harbor on December 7, 1941, Johnson's prodefense views and his support of Roosevelt's interventionist policies appeared vindicated. He immediately volunteered to go fight, as he had promised he would do in his recent campaign for a seat in the U.S. Senate. In fact, he was the first in Congress to do so. Two days later on December 9, 1941, Johnson reported to the U.S. Navy for duty as a lieutenant commander. While Johnson may have been the first on Capitol Hill to volunteer, he was hardly the last. President Roosevelt eventually had to order members of Congress who had donned the uniform to return to Washington to tend to their offices and the nation's business. Johnson, who had received (from General Douglas MacArthur, no less) the Silver Star for gallantry in action during a hair-raising aerial combat mission over New Guinea, was released from active duty on July 16, 1942. Johnson was thirty-two years old.

What is striking about Johnson's willingness to fight or, to be more accurate, to allow himself to be placed in harm's way, is that while a military-industrial complex would assume mature form during the war, forever changing the nature of the republic, the *power elite* — a term later used by the sociologist and Texan C. Wright Mills — nevertheless refused to allow themselves to be spared the consequences of their policies, unless by order of the president himself. A sense of civic duty, in other words, seized the entire nation, if only temporarily. Indeed, that Johnson and his peers in Congress were willing to put themselves in harm's way for the sake of the country helped, as much as anything else, to legitimate the government's conduct of the war, mistakes and all, in the eyes of their fellow country-men and women. Doubtless, opportunism on Johnson's part and his peers was another factor. But that the nation's leaders should see military service as a political asset speaks of just how different those times really were from our own, when the mili-tary has become an essentially European or a class-bound in-stitution, one divided between an upper-class officer corps and working-class and poor enlistees. For the Second World War was the *good* war for a reason; it was as democratic as a military institution in an advanced industrialized nation is likely to get. The ethos of shared sacrifice and a sense of common purpose inspired national confidence and instilled trust in the nation's leaders that would carry over long after the last shots of the last battle were fired. Of course, it was not just the nation's political elite who demonstrated support for the president's call to arms. Millions of citizens were determined, whether privileged or poor, to do their part as well. And those who remained on the home front nevertheless expected to do their part by paying taxes, buying war bonds, building weapons, enduring ration-ing, planting victory gardens, and making any other sacrifices deemed necessary to win the war. For once, everyone was in the same boat—except for those in the "colored only" boat, of course—and rowing toward the same shore, if one divided into segregated beaches.

If isolationism was drowned in the vast ground swell of post–Pearl Harbor patriotism, the old Nye Report suspicion of big business and those who would use their positions to prof-iteer was in no way diminished. Indeed, the U.S. Senate's Spe-cial Committee to Investigate the National Defense Program, which was chaired by Missouri Democrat and First World War combat veteran Harry S. Truman, enjoyed wide public sup-port. This committee, which was charged, in effect, with inves-

tigating the Roosevelt administration, began its work in March
1941, coincident with the passage of the Lend-Lease Act that
same month. In the end, it is estimated that the Truman Committee, in its nonpartisan investigations of the awarding and
managing of defense contracts, saved the U.S. Treasury over
$11 billion (to put this figure into context, the estimated costs
of the hugely expensive Manhattan Project, which developed
the first atom bombs, were $2 billion). The Truman Commit-
tee was a model of the American system of government at
work, and one tested by the conditions set by the most terrible
war in human history. The committee's hearings also — not surprisingly, given the healthy distrust of power on the part of
Americans at that time — served to bring Senator Truman into
national prominence (his picture made it on the cover of the
March 8, 1943, issue of *Time* magazine), and in 1944, his role as
the taxpayers' watchdog earned him a coveted place on the
Democrat's national ticket as Roosevelt's running mate. As
events in the postwar era would soon show, however, there is a
very short distance between suspecting abuse of power in high
places, a suspicion that is vital to democracy, and paranoia that
conspiracies, communist or otherwise, are afoot in the land,
weakening the country's institutions.

During the war, Johnson never wavered from his support of
Roosevelt, at least on the big things. The key to Johnson's
politics — his Texas-style liberalism — is that Johnson fully
agreed with Roosevelt that the United States had to be strong
on defense and interventionist, if necessary; he also concurred
with those in his party who believed that American power
should be used to restructure society at home, thereby saving
capitalism but at the same time ensuring that this economic
system worked on a more equitable basis. The United States
must be able to do better than to leave behind, as Roosevelt said
in 1937, one-third of its people "ill-housed, ill-clad, and ill-
nourished." The pairing of national defense — and all that this
position implies — with a commitment to social and economic
security defined the modern Democratic Party, a fact that goes
far in explaining its strong electoral appeal and decades-long

majority status. It is no easy thing, however, to be the party of both war and peace. Robert M. Hutchins, an "eastern liberal" and president of the University of Chicago, delivered a speech against lend-lease on January 23, 1941, myopically arguing that providing for security abroad would very likely mean that the promise of the New Deal would go unrealized. Citing the National Resources Board and *Fortune* magazine, Hutchins observed that "more than half our people are living below the minimum level of subsistence. More than half the army which will defend democracy will be drawn from those who have had this experience of the economic benefits of 'the American way of life.'" The resources that ought to be used to address this inequity, Hutchins feared, would be lost to war. Hutchins seemed oblivious, however, to what would be lost if totalitarianism triumphed in Europe and Asia.

Johnson's genius was in regional development. This was ever on his mind, and given his experience during the Great Depression with state-directed investment, such as bringing electricity to the Hill Country (the sine qua non of Central Texas's future), he recognized early, even before the United States was openly at war, that military spending and public investment were by no means mutually exclusive. The shift from reforms to uniforms that the war brought about meant, if anything, that there would be more federal funds available for dispersal, not less, and that given his close ties with the Roosevelt administration, he could expect to be a major conduit of those funds. Indeed, Roosevelt saw to it that his man in Texas was taken care of even as Johnson devoted his energy and talents to raising funds to help Democrats keep their majority in the House (and Sam Rayburn his position as Speaker) in the 1940 elections. And as one of Texas's major watermasters of federal largess, Johnson could expect to create entirely new constituencies dependent on him, as well as help his friends such as Brown & Root (who happily returned the favor in various indirect ways), all of which increased his own power and importance in the state as well as further adding to the power and influence of the Democratic Party.

In 1940, Johnson who was always well informed, knew that new defense plants were in the works and was already trying to steer Secretary of War Henry Stimson into building them in Central Texas because the area was "reasonably secure from long range bombing." But Johnson did not confine his efforts to his district; he worked to see that the entire state of Texas was turned into a great arsenal of democracy. He was involved in setting up the Corpus Christi Naval Air Station, which put Brown & Root in the same league as Howard Hughes and Henry J. Kaiser, as well as with the naval air training station outside Dallas and the shipbuilding facilities in Houston and Orange. Johnson also helped start ROTC units at several universities, including his alma mater in San Marcos. In short, he saw the future more clearly than most. After Pearl Harbor, Johnson would declare, "Our job is now clear. All Americans must be prepared to make, on a twenty-four-hour schedule, every war weapon possible, and the war factory line will use men and materials which will bring the war effort home to every man, women, and child in America. All one hundred thirty million of us will be needed to answer the sunrise stealth, the Sabbath day assassins."

Roosevelt's New Deal had tried, and in no small degree succeeded, in industrializing parts of both the West and the South through regional planning and federal largesse. But as Gerald Nash — one of the leading historians of the American West — argued in 1985, it was the Second World War that transformed the American West, and "no other single influence on the region — not the Mexican War, not the Civil War, not World War I, nor even the Great Depression — brought such great and cataclysmic changes to the West." Nash declared, moreover, that "In four short years the war brought a maturation to the West that in peacetime might have taken generations to accomplish. It transformed an area with a self-image that emphasized colonialism into one boasting self-sufficiency and innovation." Indeed, Nash went further and argued that the "erstwhile backward section had become a *pace-setter* [italics mine] for the nation"; thus the war not only changed but reversed the relationship between East and West. Westerners not only had good jobs but had jobs of the future in aerospace, electronics, and nuclear energy. The economies of states like California and Johnson's Texas were especially affected by the war against Nazi tyranny and Japanese militarism.

A year after Nash presented his thesis, Gavin Wright, in *Old South, New South: Revolutions in the Southern Economy since the Civil War* (1986), argued that the economic changes of the war years helped prepare the way for the civil rights movement. What Johnson seemed to understand better than most was that if promoting the common welfare invites political division, as the New Deal had proved (by 1938, opposition to FDR's policies was already well formed), providing for the common defense encourages unity. Indeed, western Democrats and Republicans were soon on board; both planned a future for their region that would involve large transferences of tax dollars from the developed eastern states to the relatively underdeveloped and strategically located western states. This was a remarkable bipartisan consensus, really, on the redistribution of the nation's wealth along clear regional lines and all in the name of national security, which, with the ensuing Cold War, continued for decades. (It should be added that this Sunbelt alliance was countered, as Boston University's Bruce J. Schulman notes, by a Frostbelt alliance in which "figures such as Senator Hubert Humphrey of Minnesota and Senator Kenneth Keating of New York" worked together to resist the West's efforts to redistribute resources by "attempting to rewrite defense procurement rules so as to benefit areas of 'chronic unemployment' — almost all of which were concentrated in the Rustbelt.")

But if this massive influx of federal monies that headed west was welcomed by the region, it was a qualified welcome given fears that corporations would, in the urgency of the moment, benefit at the expense of small business. Indeed, as it turned out, two-thirds of the wartime contracts were awarded to the country's five hundred largest corporations. Westerners such as Wyoming's senator Joseph C. O'Mahoney and Montana's senator James E. Murray worried, as Murray put it in 1941, that

"Small business for many years has been waging a losing fight against its big competitors. The growing concentration of economic control and the extension of monopolistic practices has become appalling. . . . A continuing concentration of economic power will be certain to result in an undermining of the very foundations upon which our system of free enterprise was built."

The secretary of the Interior, Harold Ickes, voiced similar concerns, warning the region in early 1942 that "Unless adequate consideration is given to these matters, the result will be that at the end of the war the people of the West will be . . . at the mercy of . . . the larger companies of the country." The solution, as O'Mahoney saw the matter, was in "the desirability of decentralizing industry." Senator Truman's special committee also took up the cause of the small businessman, keenly aware as the members were of the advantages that corporations enjoyed in obtaining defense contracts in times of national emergency.

Economic concentration and the threat it posed to free enterprise and democracy was a real problem — in the West, South, and everywhere else in the country for that matter. Self-reliance is the quintessential American ideal. But from Johnson's point of view, poverty and the crippling backwardness that comes with it, was no less a problem, for much the same reason — either way there is a loss of real independence. And without independence, a republic ceases to be meaningful in any Jeffersonian sense. Johnson knew firsthand about the diminished and damaged lives experienced by many back home in the Texas Hill Country, which the American economy had long ago passed by. And he concluded that money — concentrated, corrupting, or otherwise — was better than no money at all.

On a personal level, Johnson had come a long way since his arrival in Washington as Kleberg's secretary, and had fallen to the usual temptations: sex and money. By 1941, he was still a young congressmen, but he was nevertheless already included within the inner circles of the nation's capital and was a frequent guest of the president himself. He had come to know the powers that be by working and socializing with them. Johnson used his office to help his friends in high places, and they, through various means, helped him politically and financially. One such relationship was with wealthy newspaper publisher Charles Marsh. Through Marsh, Johnson was introduced to the English-style landed estate near Culpepper, Virginia, called Longlea. In terms of size, it was no King Ranch, but as Marsh's guest, Johnson experienced how the top 1 percent of the population lived—more so than Marsh had intended, as it turned out, for Johnson met Marsh's beautiful and elegant mistress and later wife, Alice Glass. Johnson and Glass entered into a love affair—neither Johnson's first nor his last. On the matter of women, Johnson would later boast that he enjoyed more women by "accident" than John F. Kennedy, another famous womanizer, had on "purpose."

By contrast, when it came to accepting money in return for favors, Johnson was very cautious, knowing full well the damage such revelations could do to his political career, especially if he were caught accepting oil money. His friends in high places had something just as valuable as money, however, and that was advice, which Marsh, the Brown brothers, and others were only too happy to give, and which was much more difficult, if impossible, to trace. And with insider information about real estate and other investment opportunities, including a nearly bankrupt radio station (KTBC) in Austin, which he purchased in 1943 and which his wife, Lady Bird, was to run, Johnson was eventually able to turn his modest income, and his wife's inheritance, into a real fortune. At the same time that Johnson was quietly working on achieving his own financial security, he was also settling down. In 1942, he bought a two-story home in northwest Washington, near Connecticut Avenue, and started a family, with the birth of Lynda in 1944 and Luci in 1947.

In short, there is no question that citizen Johnson personally benefited from the use of his public office and had become a textbook example of the corrupting influence of government and money. Still, if opportunistic, and sometimes crassly so— inclinations that would eventually catch up with him—he was nevertheless no sellout. He never forgot where he came from; he also never forgot how he had achieved his success, by helping capital through public policy, framed in terms of national betterment, even if these deals were first brokered in back rooms before being openly debated in the halls of Congress. And these deals arguably served the common good, since they resulted in the creation of high-paying jobs and better living standards for the people of Texas. But if Texas became all but enthralled to an emerging military-industrial complex, paid for at the U.S. taxpayer's expense, at least this circumstance seemed vastly preferable than relying on the free market to create jobs, as the 1930s had bitterly proved. It was a Faustian bargain, to be sure, but one the congressman from the Tenth District made with a firm Texas handshake and no regrets, unlike some of his other, more hesitant colleagues farther West.

The economic benefits of the war to the Lone Star State were simply enormous. In a state with a population of 6,414,842 in 1940, approximately 1,250,000 troops would be trained at Texas's fifteen army posts and forty air bases and another 79,982 German, Italian, and Japanese prisoners of war would be held in Texas POW camps. Three quarters of a million Texans would serve in World War II. All this military activity — federal payrolls, contracts, and demand — caused local business to boom in Austin, Corpus Christi, Grand Prairie, Orange, Beaumont, Port Arthur, Galveston, Houston, Lubbock, the Dallas–Fort Worth area, Midland, San Angelo, San Marcos, Wichita Falls, and perhaps no place more so than in San Antonio, with the military activity that came to be concentrated there. In addition, government orders for ships, planes, petroleum products, synthetic rubber, steel, tin, paper, lumber, and foodstuffs stimulated every sector of the state's economy. With the mechanization and increased productivity of agriculture, coupled with the high demand for labor in urban areas, the war accelerated the rural to urban shift in the state's population, a migration pattern repeated all over the country. In the long term, the sharp decline in small farmers was a key political as well as demographic development, since farmers made up an important part of the New Deal coalition, which included African Americans, urban ethnics, labor, liberals, and the Solid South.

Capital thrived in the U.S. wartime economy, with the government in some cases actually guaranteeing profits to manufacturers and builders through devices such as cost-plus contracts. Johnson had helped Brown & Root obtain just such a risk-free arrangement with its contract to build the Corpus Christi Naval Air Station. Progressive taxes and a stronger labor movement ensured, however, that the economy did not return to the dangerous imbalances and inequities of the 1920s. Moreover, the stage was being set, although few appreciated it at the time, for a major economic takeoff. In the postwar era the United States would outstrip all other economies, including those of Europe, in part because New Deal (or social democratic policies) had the effect of strengthening and expanding the middle class.

The larger story of capitalism is even more relevant to our purposes here, for no other force did more to change the United States and the world in the twentieth century. Indeed, despite two world wars and the Great Depression, from 1900 to 1950 the total output of the global economy increased in value from $2 trillion to $5 trillion. During the second half of the twentieth century, this remarkable output rose to an astonishing $39 trillion, transforming the planet's environment and diverse human society in the process. This unprecedented wealth creation and the incredible power it created led almost inevitably to conflict, because in global terms, much of this wealth and power was concentrated by region and class. Economic trends evident at the beginning of the twentieth century had by its end produced a world in which the per capita gross national income in the United States was $34,100, in Brazil $3,580, in India $450, and in Burkina Faso $210. The failure to spread the benefits of globalization evenly, or fast enough, produced cataclysmic changes. Early in the century, there were such upheavals as the Russian and Mexican revolutions; by mid-century, another world war, followed by a cold war. Although the world, even before the defeat of the Axis Powers, began dividing into capitalist and avowedly noncapitalist states, foremost amongst the latter were the Soviet Union and the People's Republic of China. This reaction to the spread of global capitalism would drive American foreign policy in the postwar era; moreover, issues of economic justice would dominate the political agenda of almost every single nation, including the United States.

Complicating this cold war from the start, however, in terms of adopting an ideologically consistent position, was the split that emerged within Roosevelt's own party over the New Deal, especially regarding the administration's limited and uneven efforts to empower workers and Americans of African descent. The reaction to these liberal reforms was strongest in the South, where, after all, a civil war had been fought in the 1860s to preserve slavery, and where racism had long been used to divide the region's poor and to disenfranchise blacks. The New Deal, in short, was undermining the South's power structure, or appeared to be threatening to do so, and in the process was turning right-wingers within the Democratic Party — W. Lee O'Daniel, Martin Dies, Eugene B. Germany, Hugh R. Cullen, Martin Dies — bitterly against their own leading standard bearer. Nowhere was this rebellion in more evidence than in Texas, which produced a political faction known as the Texas Regulars. This group of white supremacists, anticommunists, and oil and business interests (many oil men were furious at the sacrifice involved in the administration's wartime price controls) tried to throw the 1944 presidential election to Republican Thomas E. Dewey. The well-financed Regulars failed to defeat Roosevelt, who remained very popular. They then disbanded but were back right after the war to oppose Truman and his moderate liberal program, the Fair Deal, and by supporting the States' Rights, or Dixiecrat, Party, which had seceded from the main Democratic Party in 1948, prefiguring by over two decades the "Southern strategy" and realignment of the region's conservative Democrats with the Republican Party. (Before that could occur, the GOP had to change, which it did by the early 1970s as it began the slow purge of Rockefeller Republicans and other party moderates from its ranks.)

It was against this increasingly reactionary background that Johnson decided to run for the U.S. Senate in 1948. Almost immediately after Johnson's announcement, Pappy O'Daniel took himself out of the running. Johnson's main opponent in the Democratic primary, then, was Coke Stevenson, Texas's popular wartime governor. Stevenson knew nothing about foreign affairs, but he had clearly distinguished himself in the minds of voters as being antigovernment, antiunion, anti–civil rights, and anticommunist; he was for fiscal responsibility, improved highways, and better teacher salaries. Stevenson's biggest strength was in what his life and career embodied, namely, the enduring and always admirable values associated with self-reliance. Indeed, Stevenson did not owe his position in public life to anyone, anymore than did Johnson. They were both self-made men. In fact, Stevenson was born in a log cabin (in 1888) a hundred miles to the north and west of Austin (his father was a Hill Country schoolteacher and surveyor) and studied books by the campfire light. He put himself through law school and built a successful practice, went into banking (from janitor to president), and served as county judge and as a state legislator before moving into the governor's mansion in 1941. He also owned a fifteen-thousand-acre ranch at Telegraph, on the Llano River. Stevenson smoked a pipe, wore a cowboy hat, spoke little, and acted deliberately. His conservatism, marred by an ugly, if typical, streak of Texas racism (i.e., Mexicans were bad but not as bad as blacks), was a true reflection of the life he lived. It was little wonder he was held in such high regard by his fellow citizens — the white ones anyway.

Defeating Stevenson was going to require every skill and asset Johnson possessed, and then some. He gave his first campaign speech in Austin, at Wooldridge Park, on May 22, 1948, at 8:00 in the evening. Woolridge was an appropriate choice. It was Austin's first city park, it was downtown, and it was where Johnson had first campaigned for Congress eleven years before. The event thus served to remind voters of his years of public service to the state. But Texas politics had shifted sharply to the right since 1937, presaging even larger changes yet to come, and Johnson's speech reflected the new and increasingly more conservative spirit of the times.

He began with his strength, his experience in military preparedness, calling, in effect, for a new drive to mobilize in the wake of Truman's postwar policies of demobilization, reconversion, and fiscal prudence. The lesson, Johnson professed, from the two world wars was that there could very well be a third world war, and the United States should be ready this time around. Noting the power and reach of new military technologies, which obviated the geographical advantages once enjoyed by the ocean-bound United States, he supported the maintenance of the nation's surplus war plants, a dramatic expansion of air power, an army enlarged to match, and in the bright radioactive glow of the successful Manhattan Project, ever more scientific research. At the dawn of the Cold War, Johnson's response to changing international conditions was not solely to push for a stronger military. He also embraced the United Nations, the Marshall Plan, free trade, and government propaganda promoting a positive image of the United States abroad. Recalling the lessons of the 1930s, Johnson rejected appeasement on grounds that it was counterproductive: "Either we work together, and build together, to make all the World a home for freedom. Or we surrender to the Godless men in Eurasia." In addition to preparedness, Johnson supported the policy of quarantining politically diseased states. However, since he recognized that political extremism was caused, in no small part, by "war-breeding conditions," namely hunger and poverty, then these underlying issues would have to be addressed separately.

Johnson's speech led with these positions, which reflected his strengths and experience in foreign affairs, in order to underscore Stevenson's lack of the same. He thus tried to turn Stevenson's most important accomplishment, his service as Texas's governor — by definition a parochial office — into a decided disadvantage. This was a time, after all, in which the United States was asserting its leadership on the world stage, consolidating its international position, and preparing for a long fight against communism in which the very "survival of Christianity" was at stake. Thus, Johnson was telling the voters that he was the man with the experience and the vision to realize these national goals and to defend their civilization.

If Johnson could tower over his rival on the subject of military preparedness and foreign affairs, he would seemingly be in no less as strong a position on domestic affairs, given his impressive New Deal record. However, the mood of the electorate had clearly changed in postwar Texas, and Johnson's campaign distanced itself from the New Deal and staked out conservative, even reactionary positions on three key issues of the day: labor, health care, and civil rights. On labor, he had voted for Taft-Hartley and to override Truman's veto, and he thus helped roll back labor's earlier limited but real gains toward re-democratizing the economy. In fact, before his Austin audience, Johnson declared that John L. Lewis, the legendary and irascible labor leader, was "the most dangerous man in America."

On the question of health care, despite President's Roosevelt's 1943 State of the Union call for "cradle to the grave" social insurance, including the "right to adequate medical care and the opportunity to achieve and enjoy good health," goals subsequently embraced by Truman as well, Johnson parted company with his party's leadership, declaring that he wanted *no part of socialized medicine.* Ignoring the fundamental issue of a patient's ability to pay, Johnson framed the question as one of supply and demand. Here he did recognize a role for the federal government to play in terms of providing assistance to state and local communities to build more hospitals and to train more doctors and nurses. But he rejected outright the progressive alternative of establishing a comprehensive national health insurance program. Like labor and health care, race was another major postwar issue and one that would transform American life. In fact, two months following Johnson's Austin speech, President Truman would order the desegregation of the U.S. armed forces. Given Johnson's later role in the civil rights movement, however, the position he staked out on race in 1948 is striking. He began by calling the federal government's civil rights program a "farce and a sham" and an "effort to set up a police state in the guise of liberty." He reminded his audience that as a congressman he had "voted *against* the so-called poll tax repeal bill," "*against* the so-called anti-lynching bill," and "*against* the FEPC" (Fair Employment Practices Commission, created by Roosevelt through executive order in 1941 to end discriminatory hiring within the federal government and in private corporations that received government contracts). "If a man can tell you whom you must hire," Johnson explained (to the presumably largely white crowd), "he can tell you whom you can't hire." The war in Europe may have been fought against Aryan supremacy, but after the war white supremacy in the American South had once again been aroused. In this early stage of the modern civil rights movement, Johnson declared for the old order. He would later change his mind.

Johnson's conservative turn was not the only thing remarkable about this particular race for the U.S. Senate. The race, actually the race to win the Democratic primary, stood out for two other reasons as well. On the one hand, it is remembered for Johnson's pioneering use of the Bell Aircraft Corporation's 47-B helicopter, which made campaigning far more efficient and more expensive at the same time (Texas is a very big state). The "newfangled" contraption caused a sensation, and however appealing Johnson's antiworker, antipoor, and antiblack political message was to Texas conservatives, his embrace of this new technology symbolized the fact that here was a forward-looking politician from the Sunbelt ready to take on the challenges of the postwar era.

For all of Johnson's political skills and his indefatigable and innovative campaigning in the summer of 1948, there was no doubt that he was fighting an uphill battle against the taciturn, pipe-smoking Coke Stevenson. In the end, he did succeed in forcing Stevenson into a runoff election, which was a significant achievement. And here Johnson was careful not to make the same mistakes he had made in the 1941 primary contest against Pappy O'Daniel, which he lost, or was made to lose, by 1,311 votes. Instead, in what was another razor-sharp election,

Johnson made sure he reported as late as possible, but when he did it was with the narrowest margin of victory, a mere 87 votes. But unlike Johnson back in 1941, Stevenson challenged the results. What followed was an ugly court fight and game of nerves that left Stevenson angry and bitter and Johnson a physical wreck. Worse, it left Johnson, who was finally declared the winner, with the taint of illegitimacy, a suggestion captured by his new nickname, Landslide Lyndon. Sometimes he was able to joke about the primary, but at other times when the subject was raised, he revealed a side of himself that had been clearly hurt by the process. In reply to the question of who really won the primary election, Tom Miller, Austin's mayor and a Johnson supporter, frankly commented, "They were stealin' votes in east Texas. . . . We were stealin' votes in south Texas. Only Jesus Christ could say who actually won it." On November 2, 1948, Johnson went on to defeat Jack Porter, his Republican opponent, in the general election, which was a foregone conclusion. This inauspicious beginning aside, and worse for the wear, Johnson was now a U.S. senator with a ferocious ambition and something to prove.

CHAPTER 4

The Cold War West

BY THE start of the Korean War in 1950, Johnson's problem-atic Senate election was already a distant memory. There were more pressing things to consider, for the United States found itself that summer in much the same situation as it had been not quite ten years before, when it faced another aggressor in Asia. And the choices U.S. political leaders had to make in 1950 were not dissimilar to those it made in 1941, namely whether to relinquish territory—however debatable its strategic value, as was the case with the Philippine Islands—to the enemy, or heroically and grimly fight the invader, despite the fact that in Korea, the invader spoke the same language as the invaded. Defending Hawai'i was one thing. It was sovereign soil. The Korean peninsula was quite a different matter. Still, Truman invoked the need to defend the nation's vital interests in this peripheral Asian country. And war, by its very nature, stirs the emotions and can provide political leaders with the opportu-nity, if handled skillfully, to forge a deep bond with voters. Johnson understood this as well as anyone, having served in office through one war. He thus lost no time in taking full advantage of Truman's "police action" in the Asian East, not only to engage the electorate but to press for a startling vision of an American West. Indeed, Johnson's Cold War West was as grand, in its own right, as Thomas Jefferson's Empire of Lib-erty, James Polk's Manifest Destiny, Abraham Lincoln's Free Land and Free Labor, and Theodore Roosevelt's Managed Commons. And, as it turned out, Johnson's vision was no less realized.

Johnson first clearly articulated his ideas about the region's future in the speech "The West: America's Answer to Russia." He delivered it on Armistice Day in 1950, five months after the outbreak of war in Asia, to a group of college students at Texas Technological College (today's Texas Tech University) in the isolated southern plains town of Lubbock, Texas. Roosevelt had earlier, and famously, advanced the notion that America should serve the world as a great arsenal of democracy. In the postwar era, Johnson believed the country should reprise this role but play it out specifically in the American West. As a New Dealer who understood the transformative power of federal largesse and as member of the U.S. Senate Armed Services Committee, and thus privy to national security needs, Johnson fully grasped what a vigorous and indefinite prosecution of the Cold War, as outlined in the 1950 National Security Council report (the influential NSC-68, written by Paul Nitze) could mean for the development of the American West. To Johnson, this report could be turned into a blank check to underwrite regional development, and the figure he had in mind was one with many zeros behind it.

This was not Johnson's first Cold War address. On July 18, for instance, a month after the North Korean invasion of South Korea, the senator told listeners in a speech broadcast on the Texas State Network that "the Communist World of the East and the Free World of the West [were] locked in open conflict" and that this "great decision will not be reached in Korea. Korea is the first battle of a greater struggle; it will not be the last." Four months later, however, Johnson had realized that the proper response to the great struggle was a vast and permanent mobilization that would remake his American West. "Just as Russia saved herself during the German invasion," Johnson orated, "through the production of her industrial machine beyond the Urals so America can and must save herself by building a great new production strength here in the land west of the Mississippi."

Johnson was referring to the incredible Soviet wartime feat of dismantling thousands of factories endangered of being captured or destroyed by the German advance into Russia during the Second World War and the reassembly of these factories in central Asia, the Urals, and western Siberia. As Soviet historian Peter Kenez put it in his *A History of the Soviet Union from the Beginning to the End* (1999), "It turned out that the command economy, with all of its faults, suited wartime conditions. The Soviet Union in a short time managed to mobilize the entire country for the purpose of the war far more thoroughly than any other belligerent nation." Kenez goes on to note that, "By 1942–1943 Soviet factories were producing more tanks and airplanes than their German counterparts." It was also true that the Soviets were not starting entirely from scratch, since well before the war, Stalin had been pushing to industrialize this central Eurasian region.

To end the Great Depression, Roosevelt's New Deal sought to promote the economic development of the South and the West. It did so by turning the federal government into a sort of bank that nationally elected leaders could draw upon on behalf of their constituencies and thereby transfer, ideally anyway, the nation's collective wealth to the most deserving areas and projects. The outbreak of war with Japan and Germany, as Johnson correctly saw, infused even more federal dollars into these two regions. And the subsequent cold war against communism, Johnson also realized, meant a permanent mobilization, given that he believed the standoff with the Soviet Union could last as long as thirty years, or until 1980. (He was not far off the mark.)

In other words, out West, as Johnson saw it, the choice between what was called in the 1960s "guns or butter" was a distinction without a difference. The Cold War West was the New Deal changed into uniform. In the 1930s, the federal government had already assumed responsibility for regulating the country's boom-and-bust economy. In the postwar era, Washington insisted on managing world affairs and to do so placed the U.S. economy on a permanent war footing and nuclear alert. It was Johnson's genius, made plain in his address to West Texas college students, not only to understand America's changing role in the world, but to see how to make the development of the American West central to the creation of the U.S. national security state, the containment of communism, and the enforcement of the Pax Americana.

It mattered that Johnson delivered his Cold War West speech in Lubbock, Texas. Situated on the eastern edge of the Llano Estacado, near Yellow House Canyon in the midst of what was once the heart of the Comanche empire, the town was founded in 1891, but not incorporated until 1909, a year after Johnson was born. Lubbock grew slowly, and its economy was based primarily on irrigated agriculture (cotton and sorghum). World War II, however, brought dramatic change to this sleepy South Plains community. The Lubbock Army Flying School, which trained thousands of pilots (7,008 to be exact) during the Second World War, was established in August 1941 to take advantage of the superlative flying conditions the area provided. And during the 1940s, Lubbock itself—after Albuquerque, New Mexico—became the fastest growing city in the country. The population grew, in fact, from a mere 1,938 souls in 1910 to 128,068 in 1960. The air base was reactivated in 1949, following a four-year hiatus and growing international tensions, and renamed Reese Air Force Base (Reese remained open until 1997).

Eight decades separated Lubbock's incorporation in 1909 with the fall of the Berlin Wall in 1989. No less than half of Lubbock's history, in other words, beginning with the reactivation of Reese AFB in 1949, coincided with and was shaped by the Cold War. If we include the first two world wars, then a significant majority of Lubbock's history, and that of many Texas and other western communities, for that matter, was overshadowed by global war—a fact that sharply distinguishes western urbanization, given the large role military bases would play in urban development, from that of the rest of the country.

Johnson reminded his young audience of the recent wars against "the Kaiser" and "Hitler," and now with the recent outbreak of the Korean War as backdrop, of the looming threat from "Communist aggressors" who "control great armies and great land masses." In the first two world wars, Johnson lectured, the key to America's victory was the nation's "industrial might" and of its "infinite industrial capacity," which he called "the greatest peace-making weapon in the history of the human race." And Johnson went on to make the point, "The present struggle between the free nations and the Communist nations is—above all else—a struggle between two economies; two mighty production machines. Unlike the struggle with the Kaiser in 1918, unlike the struggle with the Axis in 1941, this is not a struggle in which two great armed forces will reach a final showdown on some well-defined battlefield. This is a struggle which may be decided by endurance; the economy with the greatest productive power and the greatest staying power will be triumphant."

Johnson then rhetorically queried his audience: "What does this mean for you?" And, "How do you, the people of the South Plains, fit into that picture?" He first made it clear that this production war would not involve making the kinds of sacrifices that had marked the previous world wars in terms of subordinating the civilian economy to the needs of the American war machine. The "cutback method," as Johnson called it, "in the long view . . . offers an illusion, not a solution." Johnson offered his audience a remarkably different and strikingly painless vision. "We can approach the problem directly," he said, "we can expand our productive facilities." That is, "If steel is in short supply, we can expand our steel producing facilities. If aluminum is limited, we can enlarge the facilities for producing it." And then Johnson asked, "Can we expand those facilities and still maintain a stable and prosperous economy? The record says we can. The record says we have. From 1939 to 1945, we increased our production 75 percent. At the start of the war, we had to curtail civilian production because our capacity was not increasing rapidly enough. But the fact remains that it was not the curtailment of civilian production which won the war. It was the overall expansion of our producing capacity by 75 percent."

To Johnson, production was the key. And "America's produc-

tion machine must grow," he believed, "and grow rapidly."
Johnson told his audience that "We have proved that there is no
top limit to our potential; we must translate that potential into
actual capacity." And, finally, he made his appeal to the audience: "You, here in the West, can play a decisive role in this
expanding production," for "The expansion must be, and I believe it will be, in the great American West." And then turning
to history, Johnson declaimed,

> From the days of the colonies in New England on down to
> the twentieth century, the West has been the hope and future
> of this land. The West, from the beginning of our history, has
> been the great American challenge. In the West, America
> found its early strength. In the West, America found its
> power and its maturity as a Nation. In the West today, Amer-
> ica will find its salvation. Here are the untapped resources —
> the resources to fuel and supply our expansion for the strug-
> gle with communism. Here is the space to grow. Here is the
> area [in] which a prudent nation can disperse its industrial
> machine with greatest hope for security. And here is the re-
> gion where the nation will find a people with the boldness,
> the self-assurance, the vitality, and the imagination to create a
> new and greater empire of industrial production. I tell you
> young people here especially — America's destiny is in your
> hands, and the hands of all of the youth of the West.

Calling to mind Roosevelt's famous 1940 speech, Johnson declared, "Your destiny is to build a great new arsenal of freedom
here in our native land."

In light of contemporary events and geopolitical realities — the
division of Europe, nuclear proliferation, the Chinese Revolution, Soviet recognition of the Vietminh, war in Korea — Johnson's call for creating "a new and greater empire of industrial
production" perhaps made sense. It was something, at least,
Americans could control. Such a development, however, whatever its regional benefits, exposed the nation's democratic institutions to the dangers of government waste and abuse as well as
political corruption — concerns President Dwight Eisenhower
would voice. But more than that, to sustain such a massive and

expensive effort, to institutionalize and make war mobilization permanent, meant nothing less than changing the fundamental character of the republic itself, for it is extremely difficult to nourish liberty and a standing army, a fact obvious to any student of government since the days of Oliver Cromwell; and to fast forward to the present, we have learned things since Johnson delivered his historic speech in Lubbock.

In 1998, the Brookings Institution, an independent Washington think tank, published *Atomic Audit: The Cost and Consequences of U.S. Nuclear Weapons since 1940*. Stephen I. Schwartz, the editor of the project, declared that the *Atomic Audit* "assembles . . . for the first time anywhere the actual and estimated costs of the U.S. nuclear weapons program since its inception." After four years of analyzing historical budget data, Schwartz issued the following reckoning: "Since 1940, the United States has spent almost $5.5 trillion (in constant 1996 dollars) on nuclear weapons and weapons-related programs." If the "$320 billion in estimated future-year costs for storing and disposing of more than five decades' worth of accumulated toxic and radioactive wastes" and the "$20 billon for dismantling nuclear weapons systems and disposing of surplus nuclear materials" are included, then the "total incurred costs of the U.S. nuclear weapons program exceed $5.8 trillion." Schwartz notes that this figure amounts to "almost 11 percent of all government expenditures from 1940 to 1996 ($51.6 trillion)" — a nuclear tithe, as it were. And to put these figures another way, Schwartz observes, "During this period, the United States spent on average nearly $98 billion a year developing and maintaining its nuclear arsenal."

The United States spent more in any given year, in fact, than the $87.5 billion that Congress authorized in 2004 for the U.S. wars in Iraq and Afghanistan. The only categories of spending that were larger for this period, Schwartz notes, "were nonnuclear national defense ($13.2 trillion) and social security ($7.9 trillion)." Moreover, in 1998, almost ten years after the fall of the Berlin Wall and three years before the terrorist attacks of 9/11 and the subsequent military buildup, Schwartz reported that an estimated $35 billion continued to be spent every year on nuclear weapons and weapons-related programs.

Since then, writers have found other, perhaps more compelling, ways of measuring the cost of the Cold War in terms other than dollar value. In the immediate aftermath of the Cold War, there was a burst of triumphalist literature, exemplified by Francis Fukuyama's 1989 article "The End of History?" Fukuyama, a senior State Department official, all but proclaimed a final ideological victory for those on the side of liberal democracy. Later, however, more sober, even dire views found expression. George Kennan, historian, diplomat, and the Mr. X of containment, looked back over his long and eventful life and observed in *At a Century's Ending* (1996), "So here we all stand — we of the Western World — at the end of this sad century; still partially crippled, genetically and morally, by the injuries we brought to ourselves in the two internecine wars of earlier decades, and confronted now with emerging global problems for the solutions to which neither our ingrained habits nor our international institutions have prepared us."

Derek Leebaert, in *The Fifty-Year Wound: The True Price of America's Cold War Victory* (2002), tried to tabulate the costs of the Cold War in terms of opportunities lost:

> For the United States, the price of victory goes far beyond the dollars spent on warheads, foreign aid, soldiers, propaganda, and intelligence. It includes, for instance, time wasted, talent misdirected, secrecy imposed, and confidence impaired. Particular costs were imposed on industry, science, and the universities. Trade was distorted and growth impeded. Today's national skepticism toward government "peacekeeping" is part of the Cold War price still being paid. The patriotism that followed devastation in New York and at the Pentagon is unlikely to revive earlier, more trusting attitudes.

To these international and national perspectives, Joan Didion offers a regional and at times very personal view of the Cold War's costs in *Where I Was From* (2003). Distinguishing the American West from the American South, she writes that "in the South they remained convinced that they had bloodied their land with history. In California we did not believe that history could bloody the land, or even touch it." The Cold War military-industrial complex, which insulated large segments of California's economy from the vicissitudes of the free market, did much to perpetuate the unreality that Didion found so distinctive about California. She summed it up this way: "The perfect circularity of the enterprise, one in which politicians controlled the letting of government contracts to companies which in turn utilized the contracts to employ potential voters, did not encourage natural selection." When defense contracts were cancelled in the early 1990s or companies like McDonnell Douglass moved their operations to St. Louis and elsewhere, California, Didion reported, found out what life was really like when not supported with other people's money. The adjustment was painful, even violent, marked by a terrible riot in Los Angeles, and made Spur Posse, a contemporary white middle-class teenage gang from Lakewood, a national exercise in cognitive dissonance.

John M. Findlay, author of *Magic Lands: Western Cityscapes and American Culture after 1940* (1992) and coeditor of *The Atomic West* (1998), wrote a review essay entitled "The Mobilized West, 1940–1990" for *H-West* in 2000. In this piece, he took issue with historians, who "ahistorically assume the existence of options that were not apparent to most Cold-War Americans. The nation was spending unprecedented sums during peacetime not because it was 'desirable' but in order to deal with a real enemy," namely, Joseph Stalin and Mao Zedong, and that "it is naïve to suggest that Americans could have directed their energies elsewhere." To don the accountant's green eyeshade and discuss the costs and benefits of the Cold War, Findlay argues, is to lose sight of the Cold War itself and what was really at stake. To make this point and capture the country's frame of mind in the early years of the Cold War, Findlay quotes from a speech Congressmen Henry M. Jackson (D-Washington) gave on October 9, 1951:

I confess to being struck by the irony of having to advance complicated and detailed arguments in support of an all-out atomic program. This is the best weapon we have[.] [I]t is our one real hope of deterring Stalin. It is the natural weapon of a country weak in brute manpower but superlatively strong in science and technology. How can we conceivably afford not to go all out? How can we conceivably not want to make every possible weapon we can? I believe that reasonable men can differ only on the degree of expansion that is now physically possible. In my own mind I am positive that we can immediately undertake to quintuple our expenditures on the atom to spend six billions annually. But it may well turn out that we should now increase our spending to 10 billions a year. I cannot, however, imagine any Member of this House going before his constituents and saying that he is not in favor of making every single atomic weapon it is within our power to produce.

Both the Truman and Eisenhower administrations operated under the now questionable premise that nuclear weapons were cheaper than conventional ones. In the parlance of the day, these new weapons gave "a bigger bang for the buck" or "more rubble for the ruble." At the same time, Findlay acknowledges that "Jackson was surely mindful that at least some of the vastly increased federal spending on nuclear weapons that he advocated would occur in Hanford in his home state" and that it is "worthwhile to ask how the United States and the West may have overreacted to national security threats."

What we do not know, of course, is whether the decision to "go all out" with a nuclear buildup would still have been made by Congress if the true costs had been known. In hindsight, we now see that Jackson and his colleagues, with whom he shared the power of the purse, unknowingly flew into a large and dense budgetary fogbank — a significant and disquieting fact about the workings of modern government, to be sure. But if the people's representatives failed to grasp the full enormity of the costs involved, they certainly appreciated the economic impact of annual expenditures in the range of $6 to $10 billion (in current dollars). The Manhattan Project, after all, which spawned a giant laboratory-and-bomb-making triplex with two legs in the western states of New Mexico and Washington and the third in the southern state of Tennessee, cost the United States a mere $2 billion in comparison — and that amount was spread out over the course of the war.

The creation of a national security state was new to the American experience. And in retrospect, its maintenance, which required an endless round of expenditures, provided a continuous source of funding that served as the basis for much of the West's subsequent development from colony to Sunbelt. Not only was Lubbock's World War II air base reactivated, in 1950, the World War II ordnance plant Pantex, near Amarillo, was sold to Texas Tech, and then reconverted into an assembly line for chemical explosives and nuclear warheads. Throughout the American West, old World War II sites were either reactivated or new Cold War sites built, eventually thickly covering the region in airfields, army bases, naval yards, marine camps, missile fields, nuclear test sites, proving grounds, bombing ranges, strategic mines, transportation corridors, lines of communication, laboratories, command centers, and arsenals.

As we have already seen, the architects of the Cold War West, Johnson foremost among them, had no real idea what it would cost the nation to mobilize and maintain the region in a state of constant war preparedness. In 1995, however, and well after the fact, the *Denver Post* estimated that the price tag might have come to a staggering $4 trillion in federal monies. But going in, as Johnson put it, the view was that "America cannot hope to survive if it relies on half-measures to win." Senator Jackson's question, "How can we conceivably afford not to go all out?" was especially true given the lack of intelligence U.S. policymakers had at the time about the Soviet military situation, obscured as it was behind the thick secrecy of the Iron Curtain. As Johnson himself would later lament in 1967, in defending the high costs of the space program, the intelligence boom from space photography revealed that "our guesses were way off. We were building things we didn't need to build. We were harboring fears we didn't need to harbor." Intelligence would remain problematic, despite spectacular advances, and politicians long after Johnson left office would continue to err on the side of caution and build things the country did not need and harbor fears they did not need to harbor.

There is nothing like the clarity of hindsight. In the 1950s, however, the nation's leaders clearly believed that it was better to be safe than sorry, and that in any event, while waging the Cold War would be expensive, it would not be prohibitive. Besides, few saw any real alternatives. But as much as Johnson saw that his state's economic development would benefit by Cold War spending, the old New Dealer and liberal nationalist in him nevertheless worried about the costs. He knew that the guns or butter tradeoff was very real and that leadership is about making difficult choices. In 1955, Johnson inserted for the record that the cost of the Cold War since the end of the Second World War came to $416,381,606,900. And while he did not know that crucial decisions about national defense were being made with less than accurate financial information, as Stephen I. Schwartz has revealed, he was certainly aware of the significant opportunity costs involved, a concern that would follow him for the remainder of his career in politics. On the floor of the Senate, Johnson voiced a concern shared by Eisenhower and others: "How many slums could have been cleared with that money? How many rivers could have been dammed at a fraction of that cost? How much power could have been generated to produce the goods of peace and prosperity?"

Western historians have long remarked on the paradox that despite the disproportionate share of economic benefits the American West received from Big Government during the Cold War, thanks to Johnson and others, the region nevertheless turned into a center of antistatist conservatism, a politics absolutely at variance with Johnson's liberal nationalism. In other words, the West bit the hand that fed it. Nowhere, perhaps, was this more true than in West Texas. If we take seriously, however, the worldview of West Texans, which journalist A. G. Mojtabai tried to do in her 1986 book *Blessèd Assurance: At Home with the*

Bomb in Amarillo, Texas, then this seeming paradox resolves itself. Amarillo, north of Lubbock and the campus of Texas Tech where Johnson gave his speech, was to the assembly of nuclear weapons what Detroit was to the making of automobiles. This importance is what drew Mojtabai to the Texas Panhandle and to the Pantex plant in particular. In her interviews with Pantex workers and other members of the Amarillo community, many of whom were self-declared "true believers," she found Amarillo incomprehensible unless she took into account the deeply held Christian views of the area, which she describes as "apocalyptic" and informed by "End-Time thinking." She reported: "Although End-Time thinking is by no means unique to Amarillo, it is uniquely clear here. When someone stands a few miles from Pantex, or works in a nuclear weapons plant, and declares: 'We are the terminal generation,' that assertion has a resonance it might not have elsewhere." The "prospect of all-out nuclear war and a final nuclear winter provides the secular equivalent of the born-again Christian's anticipated 'Tribulation' of the earth." In short, on the panhandle, "nuclear reality" intersected with "religious vision." In that sweeping horizontal yellow landscape, eschatology was no longer a subject of theology but an object of reality.

To Johnson, the Cold War was a means, as the Second World War and the New Deal had been before, of turning federal dollars into western development. It was a way to realize more fully in the twentieth century the country's Manifest Destiny of the nineteenth. But many of Johnson's Christian constituents did not ascribe to his liberal view and narrative of national progress. The Cold War was not another chapter of a secular story of improvement but rather the predicted reality of Revelations. Panhandle politics, in other words, was not the art of compromise but the prelude to the Rapture, which was, to quote Mojtabai further, the "divine rescue of true believers from the coming holocaust." In the end, perhaps the emergence of this militant faith—now mutated and remobilized in the wake of 9/11—rather than any sense of budgetary unreality was the significance of Lyndon Johnson's Cold War West.

CHAPTER 5

Johnson's First Mistake

DURING the 1950s, Johnson quickly emerged as one of the most powerful senators in U.S. history. Although elected to the Senate in 1948, in 1951, at the age of forty-three, he was elected by his peers to the position of majority whip; in 1953 as minority leader; and two years later as majority leader. By all accounts, he was an extraordinarily effective leader; but some, like Wisconsin's William Proxmire (who succeeded Joseph McCarthy), a fellow Democrat, would say a dominating figure. In 1960, Johnson would quit the Senate, however, to run as John F. Kennedy's vice presidential running mate, bringing Texas into the Democratic Party's column, which proved crucial in what was a very close race against Richard M. Nixon, the Republican Party's standard bearer. Johnson's decision to leave the U.S. Senate was a mistake. Unlike his career in the nation's legislature, a career marked by distinction, brilliance, compromise, and courage, his tenure in the nation's executive branch — he became president following Kennedy's assassination in Dallas, Texas, on November 22, 1963 — was troubled and tragic, however full of accomplishment and inspired by his liberal vision of a Great Society. His decision to leave the White House in 1968 was also a mistake of historic proportions, if for very different reasons.

In the wake of the Second World War, it is hardly surprising that civil rights would once again dominate American politics, the way it had in the years immediately following the U.S. Civil War and for similar reasons. The Allies in the Second World War had fought to defeat not one but two would-be master races — the Germans and the Japanese — just as Union forces in the Civil War had fought against another self-proclaimed master race. Southern elites were a race as well as a class that was trying to defend its position by means of a new political structure, the Confederacy. In the twentieth century, Adolf Hitler, Benito Mussolini, and Hideki Tōjō tried to create their own world order by means of fascist or military ideologies, war, conquest, and genocide. Thus, the issues of race and citizenship and the meaning of democracy took on a new sense of urgency in the middle decades of the twentieth century, even as nations of the world squared off to wage a long cold war, a conflict between capitalism and communism that was notably ideological rather than racial, nationalistic, or imperialistic. Certain Cold War conflicts, however, such as the Vietnam, or "American," War, were much more difficult to define.

The modern civil rights movement, then, drew inspiration from the recent Second World War, a global struggle for freedom, which had cost millions of lives and had wrecked Europe and Asia's empires as well as pretensions, while helping to turn the multicultural conglomerations of the United States of America and the Union of Soviet Socialist Republics into global hegemons. The civil rights movement was also driven, and fundamentally so, by the old Reconstruction-era dream of creating a radical biracial democracy in the South. This old, unfinished business took on new meaning during the Cold War. The intense rivalry between two competing global systems turned what had been regarded in the United States as a purely regional situation, the creation of a legal system of racial segregation, into a pressing matter of international significance.

In other words, U.S. support for the Universal Declaration of Human Rights, which was proclaimed in 1948, would somehow have to be reconciled with the recalcitrant South's simultaneous assertion of states' rights and calls for a regime of white supremacy in perpetuity. Johnson understood that the United States — as the leader of the free world — could not have it both ways. And he therefore realized that the white South, including his native Texas, like it or not, would have to change. As clearsighted as Johnson was on this point, he later proved less able to appreciate the fact that the civil rights movement had become genuinely revolutionary; that its leaders, however gifted, were following rather than leading a powerful call for change. And like any revolutionary situation, before it was over, the civil rights movement, or movements, took unpredictable, sometimes irrational, and even violent and self-destructive turns.

Still, Johnson could play the race card as well as any southern politician, using coded and not-so-coded references in support of white supremacy. In his 1948 Senate campaign, when there was a resurgence of racism across Texas and the South, Johnson stooped to such tactics in order to survive. But the Lost Cause, however much it might have been romanticized, most notably in the 1939 film *Gone with the Wind*, which portrayed a noble South as victim of northern aggression, never appealed to him, politically anyway, as it did to other southerners. Later, in 1956, many of the South's congressmen and senators, including Senator William J. Fulbright of Arkansas; Senator Richard Russell of Georgia, one of Johnson's good friends and mentors; and Senator Price Daniel of Texas, signed the Southern Manifesto, a defense of the region's racial order. Johnson's signature, however, was pointedly and conspicuously absent. And the following year, as Johnson biographer Robert Caro made clear, it was Johnson who would steer a civil rights bill to President Eisenhower's desk, legislation that Johnson called "A Great Step Forward," and the first legislation of its kind since Reconstruction.

For decades historians, writers, politicians, boosters, and the tireless Daughters of the Confederacy had tried to cast the South's defense of its slave-supported way of life in some other terms, such as white freedom, and even went to such absurd lengths as to suggest a moral equivalency between the South's secession from the Union and the North's preservation of it. The modern civil rights movement, however, had succeeded, once and for all, in removing the white hood from the South's grim and ugly past to show it for what it really was. And Johnson would play a key role in demythologizing the South, even as he exploited a mythologized West. By virtue of his Texas heritage, he was adept at playing the southern gentleman on a personal level to great political effect. In public, he could also don a Stetson, hold press conferences at his ranch on the Pedernales, and otherwise identify himself with the American West, or Texan West. This subregion west of Balcones Escarpment and extending all the way to the New Mexican border was where southerners were transformed into westerners. Although southerners had moved into other parts of the West, most recently Okies and Arkies into California, the Texan West was settled by a large influx of southerners. Johnson's own family was a case in point. So the history of the Texan West remains somewhat distinct from that of the West's other important subregions.

The Cold War, like a ball on the end of string whirling around a center, impelled the country to look ever outward, while the civil rights movement, like the string on which the ball was tied, had the opposite effect, compelling the country to turn inward and reexamine its past. During the 1950s, these powerful centrifugal and centripetal forces in American politics somehow served to balance each other, giving that decade an uneasy sense of equipoise, all the more so if contrasted with the convulsions that came in the 1960s. Underpinning the apparent stability of this period was Johnson himself, now the most important Democrat in Washington. His moderate liberalism played perfectly against the moderate conservatism of President Dwight Eisenhower, who defeated the Illinois Democrat Adlai Stevenson in 1952 and again in 1956. Johnson and Eisenhower both knew how to run things, and in fact enjoyed and took pride in running things; having been schooled in depression and war, they saw government as a constructive and positive force in the life of their country. They were the right men, in the right place, at the right time.

In 1951, the same year Johnson was elected majority whip, and twenty years after he first came to Washington, D.C., as Congressman Richard Kleberg's secretary, Johnson purchased property along the Pedernales River, a place within walking distance of where he was born. It was no King Ranch but there was enough land on which to raise cattle. Johnson was not interested in Herefords as an economic proposition, of course; his interest was in raising votes. He recognized the ranch's potential as political symbol and theater. He had come to understand the appeal of the western myth; he had witnessed the response of voters to the cowboy politicians, Kleberg and more recently Coke Stevenson. The LBJ Ranch also represented Johnson's financial independence, which he had achieved through his Austin media interests.

The postwar era was a time when Americans were on the move. Congress, building on previous New Deal highway legislation, passed the National Interstate and Defense Highways Act of 1956, providing for a transcontinental system of super highways, which would transform the nation's transportation system and further integrate the American West into the U.S. economy. During this period, millions moved West in a second great western migration, producing what journalist Neil Morgan called in 1961 the "westward tilt" of the nation's population. In this modern-day western movement, Americans drove in gasoline-powered station wagons rather than in horse-drawn prairie schooners. Even those who did not go west were moving from cities to newly built suburbs. Here, on the crabgrass frontier, many bought western- or ranch-style homes. Johnson's acquisition of a ranch reflected these national trends. If all this were not enough, everyone who could afford a television set watched, and seemed to enjoy, an endless parade of westerns — one-horse operas and simple morality tales that reinforced cherished ideas about independence, freedom, and living close to the land.

The myth of the Old West resonated in Johnson's Hill Country as well as in the rest of Texas, and, significantly, the Old West, like the South's Lost Cause, was something that could be turned into votes. While the Old West had a local appeal as a region of the imagination and one free of sectional strife and racial division, it had also been nationalized. It was no accident that what would become the first edition of Ray Allen Billington's classic textbook *Westward Expansion: A History of the American Frontier* was published in 1949, at the onset of the

Cold War. Billington's text was based on the famous thesis of Frederick Jackson Turner, an American historian of the late nineteenth and early twentieth centuries, who argued that taming the western frontier was the process that made Americans distinctly American—a message endlessly echoed in motion pictures, television shows, pulp magazines, on vinyl records, and in secondary and college classrooms. Indeed, the frontier thesis became the unofficial creation myth of the nation for the duration of the Cold War. As nationalistic and ethnocentric as this idea was, it nevertheless did not preclude an appeal to a larger, if weaker, sense that Americans also belonged to a western civilization—styled the "free world" after the Second World War—which they now found themselves not so reluctantly forced to defend. So alongside Billington's textbook of frontier history were Western Civilization textbooks, to support the course Western Civilization, a curricula mainstay dating back to the First World War. Thus, America's rapidly growing number of college students, who would play such a vocal and visible role in the next decade, were offered a sometimes complementary, sometimes contradictory vision of the nation's unique past but shared place in the world.

Moreover, Turner had succeeded in turning the frontier, which was known to his contemporaries through entertainments such as dime novels and Wild West shows, into a scholarly subject; by the mid-twentieth century, artists, writers, musicians, directors, and actors had succeeded in turning frontier scholarship back into entertainment, but one with serious political overtones, thus rounding the circle. This creative back and forth between myth and reality, with each informing and imbuing the other, would eventually become stifled, however, as the story of the frontier movement became ossified as Cold War ideology. Moreover, the very morality of America's westward expansion came into question with what seemed to be the story's violent and tragic denouement, America's war in Vietnam.

In the 1950s, America's Asian Götterdämmerung was still far off, although in retrospect, France's failure in Indochina to restore its colonial empire seemed to prefigure America's own military experience in Southeast Asia a decade later. During the fighting of the First Indochina War, Johnson had been opposed to U.S. military intervention in Vietnam unless it was carried out in cooperation with allies and the French promised independence to its former colony. In 1954, the Vietminh delivered a decisive defeat to France's forces at Dien Bien Phu, a remote mountain outpost near the Laotian border. With France unable to impose its will on the north, and Ho Chi Minh's Vietminh too weak to exert control over the south, the country was at an impasse, and Vietnam's fate was left to the diplomats. Under the Geneva Accords, the S-shaped country was to be reunited in two years with the elections of a single, national government. In the meantime, Vietnam's situation invited comparison with the formal division of Korea of the year before and to a lesser extent with the earlier division of Germany.

But in Korea and Germany the United States had fought and bled for territory it now claimed on behalf of the free world and sought to defend against further aggression through friendly governments and, to a lesser extent, through the support of local populations. The situation in Vietnam appeared deceptively similar to these other two national catastrophes. Vietnam's predicament even started to resemble the recent partition of India into Muslim Pakistan and Hindu India, when a million Catholics streamed south across Vietnam's seventeenth parallel in fear of living under communist rule. Thus, there was an important difference between Vietnam and its Cold War counterparts, Korea and Germany: the United States, although it provided France with military aid, lacked the moral authority and influence that it enjoyed in South Korea and West Germany.

President Eisenhower and Secretary of State John Foster Dulles did find a man with whom they thought they could work, the aristocrat, Christian, and patriot (he had not collaborated with the French) Ngo Dinh Diem. Washington's new man (who proved to be no puppet and was as authentic a leader and Vietnamese as any communist from the North) in turn canceled elections scheduled for 1956, as provided by the peace accord, denying otherwise certain political victory to Ho

Chi Minh, a staunch Stalinist, fervent nationalist, and a tenacious but capable and inspirational leader. Ho Chi Minh enjoyed widespread popular support. Diem and Ho Chi Minh both saw themselves as Vietnam's true leader. When the United States backed Diem, however, it took sides in what was as yet an undeclared civil war over the future of the country, since neither side was interested in seceding from the other. Only the Americans considered South Vietnam's independence a viable option, which was ironic given their own history but may be explained by their recent experiences with secession in Korea and Germany. A half a loaf is better than no loaf, after all. In the meantime, Ho Chi Minh followed Stalin and Mao, believing as they did that a backward, agrarian state could condense the nineteenth century's transportation and communication revolutions in a five-year plan or two and be rapidly turned into a modern, industrialized nation.

For poor and backward countries, communism had enormous appeal because it promised something for nothing, and it worked like a great pyramid scheme. There was the initial quick return that came with attacking the successful and redistributing land and wealth, an action that also had the political benefit of destroying the economic base of a potential opposition movement and rendering the population dependent on a one-party state. But once class or neighbor envy had been satisfied and old scores settled, there was little left to look forward to except the tasteless cream of collectivization and the bleak and dreary uniformity of communist life.

In a remote sense, this supposed fast track to modernization was an extremely crude version of Johnson's own efforts to develop and integrate the regional economies of the American South and West through massive public investment, wealth that originated in the nation's rich industrial and urban centers, far from the hardscrabble farms and ranches of the Texas Hill Country. Johnson was successful because, as the old saying goes, you need money to make money, and Johnson always knew where the money was. Moreover, he supported reinvesting the nation's wealth to make more wealth rather than merely redistributing it. The Great Depression also was a painful reminder of the damage that plutocratic excess can do to an economy. The senator from Texas thus had the moral argument of fairness and justice on his side to use the federal government to spread around some of this piled-up wealth to places and people where it could do some good; to bypass the badly clogged arteries, as it were, and get the blood of the U.S. economy freely circulating again to every part of the body. And he made this happen by being connected to virtually every piece of legislation taken up by the U.S. Senate in the 1950s. And his efforts worked, as a Sunday drive from Austin south to San Antonio would one day prove.

After France's defeat, the communists in Vietnam embraced land reform, which might have had some political benefits had it been competently carried out, as was the case in Mexico. There, south of Johnson's Texas, Lázaro Cárdenas broke up the *latifundios* and efficiently redistributed the land to the country's dispossessed, even as he successfully nationalized Mexico's oil, old solutions that only partially addressed new and changing economic and social conditions. In Vietnam, as was the case in Mexico, the reality of land reform differed sharply from the promise, for at the end of the day, the countryside—whether it was owned by one avaricious landlord or divided equitably to all the virtuous peasants—could produce only so much rice or catfish. These commodities in turn could only be sold, traded, credited, or exchanged. There would never be enough economic activity—based on raising agricultural commodities alone—to generate the capital necessary to finance the North's modernization and build a modern socialist society. To this day, in fact, Vietnam remains one of the poorest countries in Asia. In the South, Diem subsequently implemented his own land reform program. This reform was limited, however. It might have made some difference in the countryside, but its failures made enemies who could look to friends in the North for support. Indeed, Diem proved to be anything but a reformer, which helps explain his anticommunism, which in turn helps explain his appeal to, and the support he received from, Eisenhower and Dulles. But the growing unpopularity of Diem's rule, abundantly manifest by the end of Eisenhower's second term, was a problem that the former supreme allied commander in Europe left for his successor, a former navy lieutenant and commanding officer of PT-109, John F. Kennedy.

On September 9, 1957, President Eisenhower signed into law the Civil Rights Act of that year, Johnson's impressive legislative achievement. It was important not in terms of the law's effectiveness — it was a very weak measure — but that it passed at all, given the deep suspicions of right-wing southern senators. These men were as little inclined to reform as were Ngo Dinh Diem and his supporters in South Vietnam. Having worked so hard on passing legislation that shook the foundations of his own party, Johnson took extra pains to mend fences and look for new support.

Looking ahead at the 1960 presidential election, Johnson tried to expand the party's appeal in the American West. He spoke to the Western States Democratic Conference, which met at the Western Skies Hotel in Albuquerque, New Mexico. The speech he gave, which went through a number of revisions, provides clear insight into what the West meant to him. Not surprisingly, Johnson made frequent references to the frontier, western expansion, and pioneer values. This was the conventional interpretation of the region and would have been universally understood by a generation of Americans raised on western films, television shows, and music. It was hardly an accident, for instance, that one of the main fantasies at Walt Disney's relatively new Anaheim amusement park was Frontier Land. But Johnson's remarks also revealed a firm grasp of another, less familiar West. This was not Turner's West; this was Walter Prescott Webb's West, which Webb discussed in his article "The American West: A Perpetual Mirage," published by *Harper's* in 1957. Here, Johnson's fellow Texan plainly declared that the West was at heart a desert.

To Johnson and other western leaders, this incontrovertible fact of geography and climate was a challenge that had already been taken up in spirit. As Johnson put it in one version of the

Lady Bird Johnson and Senator Lyndon B. Johnson in 1934 Ford Phaeton, parked on a Pedernales River dam, water cascading around them, 1959. (LBJ Library, Pre Pres Collection)

speech, "Every day when my fellow Texan—Speaker of the House Representatives Sam Rayburn—goes to his rostrum in the House—he sees inscribed on the wall [behind] his chair, the following quotation: *Let us develop the resources of our land—call forth its powers—build up its institutions—promote all its great interests—and see whether we also in our day and generation may not perform something worthy to be remembered.*" For Johnson, water reclamation had long been part of the Texas gospel. He was in the Rio Grande Valley, that long green ribbon in an otherwise sere landscape, to spread the word among politicians already largely converted. The question had been settled long ago as to whether the region's resources would be developed and that Washington would have to play a leading role in their development. This was part of the nation's unfinished business. What remained to be determined was which party — the Democrats or the Republicans — would do a better job of working with westerners to ensure the region reached its full economic potential.

Johnson had mastered the arguments of economic, or liberal, nationalism, a belief that had animated much of Roosevelt's New Deal. Johnson had also learned how to use the need to compete with the Soviet Union to leverage federal funds to his home state. He had no difficulty expanding this Cold War rhetoric to include the American West. Johnson noted that the Soviets boast of "irrigating deserts by the wise use of atomic energy," whereas the Eisenhower administration declares "no new starts." How can we sit by, Johnson implored in one version of his Albuquerque speech, while "The world is being told that the leading nation of communism is seeking to build, to construct, to plan for the future. At the same time, it is being told that the leading nation of freedom is seeking to constrict, to cut down, to return to the past. The communists boast of the things they are doing. We boast of the things we cannot afford to do." It was no less than our patriotic duty, Johnson seemed to be saying, to develop the waters of the West. And if the point was lost on anyone, he explicitly declared, "There are direct parallels between our water resources program and our position of world leadership." An ancient Mesopotamian king, whose power was ultimately derived from the mastery of irrigation, would have nodded in agreement as he would have understood the relationship between the two.

Goading the party in power, in this case the Republican Party, for not doing enough to meet external threats was easy to do, for when it comes to securing lives and property, when is enough really enough? This line of attack is an almost irresistible temptation for politicians in the opposition and marks one of the weaknesses of the U.S. democratic process, for there is really no penalty for outbidding your opponent. Eisenhower had correctly assessed the risks to the nation and wisely pursued a middle course, leaving the country secure and solvent. But these policies, however sound, would leave Vice President Nixon, the Republican Party's presidential nominee, vulnerable to attack. He had to defend Ike's moderation against those who claimed the country could do better. If one million bombers, guns, helmets, or bullets are good, then who would argue with one million *plus one,* and so on. Johnson and the Democrats grasped this opening and exploited it fully, smartly exploiting the Soviet satellite *Sputnik* and crying there was a "missile gap," even as Eisenhower warned the country in his farewell address against the military-industrial complex, bringing to mind, per-haps for older voters, the "merchants of death" about whom Gerald Nye and an earlier generation of Americans had fretted.

The presidential election of 1960 returned the Democrats to the White House after an eight-year hiatus. The contest be-tween John F. Kennedy, who won, and Richard Nixon was very close but was interesting in other ways as well. It was a contest between a New Englander, Kennedy, a very rich Irish Catholic who was nevertheless seen in every other respect as a WASP, and Richard Nixon, a Californian, who had worked his way up from far more humble circumstances, having none of the ad-vantages of great family wealth that had been bestowed on Kennedy. As for religion, Nixon was a Quaker but was any-thing but a pacifist or consensus builder. Kennedy also had an incredibly important asset: his brother Robert, who was no less able and fiercely loyal. With such support, along with winning qualities and a keen political ambition, one could go far in life, and Kennedy went as far as one could go. Nixon reached the same mountaintop eight years later, but the trail he took was much more circuitous and difficult. Nixon was very intelligent, quite shrewd, and possessed of genuine vision, at least a strate-gic vision—a rare thing, actually. But he was a badly flawed human being. Despite his many accomplishments, including having been twice elected vice president of the United States, he remained insecure, a trait he wore like a cheap suit all his life, a trait which ultimately proved to be his undoing.

Kennedy had yet another major advantage: Lyndon John-son, who agreed to serve as Kennedy's vice president. As a man who had always looked to senior men for advice, support, and help to the next plateau, this was a major role reversal for John-

Senators Kennedy and Johnson enjoying a light moment during their
1960 campaign. (George Mason University)

son. What the younger and less experienced Kennedy wanted was clear — Texas and the South brought into the Democratic column on election night. What Johnson wanted was eventually the presidency, and this was one way to overcome his regional disadvantage and the difficulty of running for the presidency from the U.S. Senate, a handicap his Massachusetts running mate was determined to overcome. But it meant that Johnson had to give up everything he had worked very hard for in the U.S. Senate. He was one of the most powerful men that body had ever produced, and he was willing to give all of this up basically for a chance to be his party's nominee for the top job in 1968. Since he certainly could not run against Kennedy in 1964, he would have to wait for eight long years. An awful lot could happen in that time, and there were no guarantees. In the meantime, he would hold a position that his fellow Texan John Nance Garner had famously valued as "not worth a bucket of warm spit." It was a curious decision. Johnson was a man who had already had one heart attack. His health was a real issue. And he would be seen as the pedestrian Truman to the more illustrious Roosevelt. That would be hard to endure — and it was. This move turned a powerful Texan into a national contender for the White House. Still, it was a big sacrifice for someone as action driven as was Johnson, and in the final analysis, it meant leaving the Senate, where he had proved himself particularly well-suited, to try to go to the White House, where he remained untested. In retrospect, the decision was a mistake.

Taking no chances, Johnson ran in two elections in 1960: one to keep his Senate seat and the other as vice president. On election day, either way, he was going to wake up a winner. As it turned out, the Kennedy-Johnson ticket narrowly defeated Nixon and his running mate, Henry Cabot Lodge. Johnson, the most powerful man in the U.S. Senate, resigned to serve as junior partner in the New England firm of Kennedy and Kennedy, which hung up its shingle at 1600 Pennsylvania Avenue. As vice president, Johnson was kept busy. He served in the cabinet and on the National Security Council during a particularly tense time in U.S.–Soviet relations, especially given the looming crisis over the placement of Soviet missiles in Castro's Cuba. He chaired the National Aeronautics and Space Council, at a critical stage in NASA's early development, as the agency oversaw the Mercury program and prepared to put a man on the earth's moon before the end of the decade, before the Soviets had a chance to do the same. This was the perfect job for a man who had said he did not want to go bed by the light of a communist moon.

Johnson also chaired President Kennedy's new Committee on Equal Employment Opportunity, out of which Johnson would come, by 1965 and as president of United States, to order a shift in the government's policy of antidiscrimination (dating back to Franklin Roosevelt's administration) to one of affirmative action. This was Johnson trying to outdo, in this case, Martin Luther King, Jr.'s call in 1963 to judge Americans not "by the color of their skin, but by the content of their character." King was an African American leader who—like César Chávez, a Mexican American leader from the fields and orchards of California—was influenced by Gandhi, a political and spiritual figure of Himalayan stature. King tried, as did Chávez, to follow Gandhi's philosophy and translate his successful tactics of nonviolent protest against the British Raj to the American situation. But in outdoing King, LBJ actually sharply broke from the soaring oratory of King's "I Have a Dream" speech. Affirmative action and other explicitly race-conscious policies ensured, by their very nature, that race would remain a divisive issue for decades to come. Although the goal was integration, a true melting pot, this fairly radical policy (affirmative action) awkwardly complemented the shift that was occurring, as the newer left abandoned the older left's dream of integration for a vapid multiculturalism, paralleling the growing attacks on conformity and the drift toward counter-culture alternatives.

The Peace Corps was yet another Kennedy initiative and part of his vision of a New Frontier. To promote peace and understanding between the United States and other countries, especially countries in Asia and Africa, this new agency tried to help the postcolonial world meet the demand for trained workers.

While the Peace Corps certainly had propaganda value for the United States, it also did real good in the world and drew thousands of sincere and idealistic young Americans into its service. Of all of the New Frontier programs, the Peace Corps perhaps best exemplified Kennedy's famous entreaty for Americans to ask not what their country could do for them, but what they could do for their country. Johnson, along with many other Americans, especially young Americans, warmly embraced the president's idealism.

The Kennedy years were brief, ending as they did with the young president being shot to death as his motorcade moved through the streets of downtown Dallas. The shooting in the city's Dealey Plaza shocked the world. Much has been written about this tragic day in Texas. It was hard to grasp that the assassin, a man who had done so very little with his own life, could take the life of someone who had succeeded in doing so much with his. The absurdity defied easy acceptance, something made even more difficult when the gunman was himself killed two days later. Not a few believed the slain president must have been the victim of a conspiracy, grand or otherwise. The Warren Commission, however, concluded that there was indeed a lone gunman. And as for the actual execution of the deed itself, there was little mystery involved. The gunman's perch on the sixth floor of the Texas Book Depository offered a clear line of sight to the street below, where the president's slow-moving, open-topped limousine passed by. Lee Harvey Oswald, the assassin, was a former U.S. marine; he had been trained how to shoot to kill. The dramatic events of the next few days gripped the nation until Kennedy was laid to rest at Arlington National Cemetery, a place marked by an eternally burning flame, and Vice President Lyndon Johnson assumed the presidency.

Johnson had left the Pedernales for the Potomac numerous times but never under such circumstances as these, never with such expectations. He handled this extremely difficult transition brilliantly, revealing his razor-sharp skills, honed after decades in politics. It was perhaps his finest moment. The country knew that the new man at the helm possessed a vast fund of experience in government upon which to draw and was distinguished by a truly remarkable record of legislative achievement, including the Civil Rights Act of 1957 and the National Aeronautics and Space Act of 1958. There was never a question whether Johnson could captain the ship of state, only where he would take it. Friends and critics alike knew that Johnson was a man who understood how Washington worked, how the sausage was made, perhaps better than anyone in the twentieth century, and thus it was clear that Johnson would be, unlike his mourned but less accomplished predecessor, a major force with whom to reckon. Johnson was certainly not the founders' idea of a leader—a man who came to public life after achieving, through his own merit, a position of wealth, independence, and respect. No, Johnson had turned this ancient formula for success precisely around. But there was something to be said even for that, for his sheer daring, audacity, and ambition. Either way, Johnson was the single most qualified man in the country to serve as president. And this lion was in charge.

In remarks he made to a group of governors on November 25, 1963, the new president stated simply, "I think continuity without confusion has got to be our password and has to be the key to our system." Johnson read the mood of the country perfectly and struck the right tone with his speech, manner, and deeds. He did blunder in not replacing key Kennedy men, such as Robert McNamara, with his own. Johnson could have given the country continuity without keeping on Kennedy's people. And indeed he did effectively move Kennedy's legislative agenda through Congress, where it had previously stalled due to the intransigence of southern Democrats. Kennedy had become a martyr to his own cause, and Johnson took full political advantage of the sympathy the country now felt for their fallen president. Johnson also possessed his own liberal vision for the country and a fierce ambition to out–New Deal the New Deal, a vision he would try to realize against the backdrop of unprecedented economic prosperity as opposed to the Great Depression faced by Roosevelt. Indeed, Johnson—LBJ—would quickly transform Kennedy's New

Frontier into the Great Society, a program that, remarkably, he saw largely enacted into law, as perhaps only he could have done.

Affluence, a product of the postwar boom, was not the only important difference between the liberal reforms of the 1930s and those of the 1960s, although it does much to explain the successes of the Great Society as well as its undoing. For Roosevelt, saving capitalism and building a strong middle class were the greatest challenges before the nation, noting as he did that the living conditions of one-third of the nation were unacceptable. That was a dangerously high percentage and it had to be addressed. In Europe and Asia, such percentages, and the widespread insecurity they represented, could and did fuel destabilizing political movements, and help explain the powerful attraction of communism and fascism, the twentieth century's famous shortcuts to power and wealth, which turned out to be dead ends or worse. But if class figured large in the New Deal, race and gender would be largely absent from Roosevelt's broad policy concerns. But certainly the future could be glimpsed in A. Philip Randolph's threat to march on Washington in 1941 unless the Roosevelt administration met the labor leader's demand to end employment discrimination.

As Johnson looked ahead to the presidential race of 1964, he was preparing to deal with a nation at a very different place in history, a superpower locked in a potentially catastrophic cold war that was also simultaneously undergoing profound social and demographic changes at home, although just how disruptive these changes would be was hardly apparent in late 1963. In fact, with the civil rights acts of 1964 and 1965, which Johnson helped make law, the black civil rights movement for full equality appeared at long last close to achieving its goals — a movement begun over a century before with the *Dred Scott* case of 1857, and which took a terrible civil war and two reconstructions, or armed interventions, to accomplish (the first after the Civil War; the second after World War II, when Eisenhower ordered troops into Little Rock, Arkansas, in 1957, to uphold *Brown v. Board of Education of Topeka*). Moreover, the issue of racial equality was seen as largely a regional issue. The noted southern historian C. Vann Woodward, however, pointed out that troubled race relations were actually a national problem, citing the 1965 Watts Riot in California as a case in point. Still, in political terms, the civil rights movement would have the greatest impact in the southern states, as opposed to states such as North Dakota, Idaho, or Arizona, where the black population was relatively small. Indeed, the civil rights movement unintentionally and ironically helped produce a major political realignment in which the Grand Old Party was to gain large purchase over a section of the country that had once taken up arms against Abraham Lincoln's government and his despised party.

Johnson also seemingly took the existence of a strong middle class for granted, the great success story of the past thirty years, and focused his gifts of persuasion not only on race but on ending poverty as well. These were compelling causes that deeply moved millions of Americans. The determination of a few to right old wrongs can be irresistible to the many. However, guilt or altruism is difficult to sustain as a political movement. Indeed, Johnson's actions helped set in motion a backlash that would drive away the very people, aspiring white working-class Americans, whom Roosevelt had earlier won over to the Democratic Party.

The demographic changes that occurred in the postwar era, known in popular shorthand as the baby boom, also distinguished the reforms of the sixties from those of its New Deal predecessor. For one thing, Americans of Roosevelt's day found their generation challenged by the generation coming of age during the Kennedy and Johnson years. The generational balance of power had not only tipped in the young's favor but produced a youth culture all its own, fueled in no small part by the fear of getting killed in a distant and abstract war. The prospect of a grim and empty death in the rice paddies and jungles of Southeast Asia, for a people with whom Americans possessed no historical ties, helped unite a generation of young men and women much as the experience of depression and war had united the generation of their parents, both with starkly different results and producing very different attitudes on everything from sex and music to government and patriotism. Johnson found himself on the wrong side of this divide, as did others. Many young Americans felt so emboldened by events that they questioned his authority by taking to the streets. Their lives or the lives of their peers depended on it. Many parents and their peers found themselves put on the defensive by the massive antiwar demonstrations of the era and the counterculture that emerged as a colorful, if failed, alternative to mainstream American life. Naturally enough, all of this in turn created anger, resentment, and feelings of disgust and envy. It was an unsettling time all the way around.

On May 22, 1964, when Johnson addressed the University of Michigan, the problems related to the generation gap appeared very far away. He spoke with a national voice, which he had found thirty years ago in Roosevelt's Washington. "For a century," he intoned, "we labored to settle and to subdue a continent. For half a century, we called upon unbounded invention and untiring industry to create an order of plenty for all of our people. The challenge of the next half century is whether we have the wisdom to use that wealth to enrich and elevate our national life, and to advance the quality of our American civilization."

In addition to eradicating poverty and racial injustice, Johnson proposed to direct this wealth to save the nation's cities, protect the environment, and improve the schools. Since the Second World War, American cities had undergone a major transformation as industries and residents, many white, migrated to the suburbs, taking with them high-paying jobs and a huge tax base. Left behind was a decaying urban core and infrastructure as well as ghetto neighborhoods. Johnson's Great Society attempted to reverse this historical trend by doing everything except what would have worked, exacting a stiff energy tax on the cheap oil that made this population shift economically possible in the first place.

The ongoing industrial revolution, which had done so much to elevate U.S. living standards and turn the nation into a superpower, had also degraded the air and water and damaged the ecosystem. Johnson's administration took the conservation of natural resources seriously and furthermore supported efforts to preserve the country's pristine rivers, forests, and deserts. LBJ saw himself as a friend of the environment, and his legislative contribution in this regard ranks in importance with those of the two Roosevelts. Finally, as a former schoolteacher and principal, LBJ had a grasp of education unique among twentieth-century presidents. He understood that the key to educational reform was better teacher training, smaller class sizes, improved facilities, and financial aid.

Speaking to the critics of expanded national power, which such an ambitious program would certainly entail, Johnson conceded, "The solution to these problems [did] not rest on a massive program in Washington, nor [could] it rely solely on the strained resources of local authority. They require[d] new concepts of cooperation, a creative federalism, between the national capitol and the leaders of local communities." Johnson then quoted Woodrow Wilson, a former U.S. president and great American nationalist second only, perhaps, to Theodore Roosevelt: "Every man sent from his university should be a man of his Nation as well as a man of his time." In a single speech in late May before an Ann Arbor audience, Johnson had clearly articulated his liberal nationalist position and defined himself to voters in the contest ahead for the presidency, scheduled six months away.

Johnson's nomination was taken for granted, and the drama went to the Republicans as they struggled over whether to nominate a moderate or a genuine conservative. In the end, after Nelson Rockefeller, governor of New York, gave Barry Goldwater a real fight in the Republican primaries, the GOP sided with the U.S. senator from Arizona, an outspoken and bona fide conservative, signaling a major change in the country's politics. The nation was thus presented in 1964 with a contest between two westerners, a Texan and an Arizonan, which showed that the American West had finally come of age in the nation's politics.

Goldwater — square jawed, forthright, and decent — was

President Lyndon B. Johnson (left) and Vice President Hubert Humphrey (right) on the LBJ Ranch, 1964. (LBJ Library, WHPO Collection)

given to blunt, impolitic public remarks that served him well in his home state and in the Senate but were easily used against him in the much larger national arena. He distinguished himself from other Republicans by his strong emphasis on the threat of tyranny at home and appeasement abroad as the major problems with which Americans had to contend. Under the administrations of Kennedy and Johnson, the country had been left, he declared, to "stagnate in the swampland of collectivism" and to "cringe before the bullying of Communism." And at the Republican National Convention in San Francisco, Goldwater ended his acceptance speech of his party's nomination with the words "Extremism in the defense of liberty is no vice. Moderation in the pursuit of justice is no virtue." Such statements were pure rhetorical hyperbole but matched the racist and warmongering charges and other equally gratuitous nonsense that came out of LBJ's cutthroat campaign. The relatively high moral tone of postwar politics, the McCarthy era notwithstanding, had been finally spent.

In November, Johnson won and won big. Goldwater won his home state and the Deep South, while Johnson raked in the remaining states. He was the incumbent and had skillfully taken over the administration of a fallen president; he had the years of experience under his Texas belt and was indeed one of the most accomplished politicians of the day, a real giant who dwarfed Goldwater in this respect. Reviewing their résumés side by side reveals simply no comparison between the two men. But if the election of 1960 left observers, such as sociologist Daniel Bell, wondering if the end of ideology was nigh, the election of 1964 suggested quite the opposite, unleashing as it did extremism on both sides. It was not clear yet that that the political center was gone, but civility in the nation's public discourse certainly seemed to be, although the presidential campaign of 1964 would pale in comparison to the vituperation that spewed forth four years later from every point on the political spectrum.

CHAPTER 6

The Seven Cities of Cíbola

THE myth of the Seven Cities of Cíbola, as reported by Cabeza de Vaca and Fray Marcos de Niza, propelled Francisco Vázquez de Coronado to explore the Southwest and Texas in the mid-sixteenth century. The search for these fabled cites of wealth, where the advanced arts were practiced, proved futile. The con-quistador's spirit broken and his flesh weak, Coronado even-tually returned to Mexico City, a failure, if a magnificent one, a New World Don Quixote. Still, the attempt to find this fantasy had taken the Spanish where they had never been before and had made them greater for it; and one day a rich civilization indeed would be built in these northern reaches that would far surpass anything the fevered imagination of the plumed knights could have ever conceived. But this would take time, a lot of time, and a lot of very hard work. Johnson, like the Spanish of old, was in a terrible hurry. He wanted to see his dream of a Great Society realized as fast as bills could be passed into law, the funds appro-priated, and the manpower gathered together to carry out the numerous projects he had in mind. Like a Texas hailstorm, Great Society programs fell fast and furious from the sky, covering the plains in white; some of these balls of hail were large and endur-ing, but many others melted away just as fast, once the sun returned overhead.

Foremost among the mixed legacies of Johnson's Great So-ciety was his commitment to ending racial injustice. To this end, the passage of the landmark civil rights acts of 1964 and 1965, as well as 1968, in which LBJ's support was instrumental, were certainly crucial in barring discrimination in the work-

L-R: Muriel Humphrey, Vice President Hubert Humphrey, President Lyndon B. Johnson, Lady Bird Johnson, Lynda Johnson, and Luci Johnson stand before crowd on inauguration night, 1965. (LBJ Library, WHPO Collection)

place, classroom, and voting booth. Changing laws was not easy. But it would prove a lot easier than changing society or a culture. In a commencement address Johnson gave at Howard University on June 4, 1965, two months before he signed the Voting Rights Act, Johnson looked ahead at this much more difficult challenge. He declared that freedom alone was not going to be enough to solve the problem of black poverty. The War on Poverty was at the heart of Johnson's Great Society. However, before the audience seated on the quadrangle in front of the library, he frankly declared that "negro poverty" was "not white poverty." True, he said, "many of its causes and many of its cures are the same," but there were also real "differences — deep, corrosive, obstinate differences — radiating painful roots into the community, and into the family, and the nature of the individual."

More specifically, the disproportion of poor blacks to middle-class blacks was certainly one crucial difference. Johnson also noted the growing concentration of poor blacks in northern ghettos, where they lived as a people apart. These numerous, if separate, communities were often located in neighborhoods once known for their vitality — such as Harlem — but now had become synonymous with violence and crime. Moreover, these neighborhoods had physically declined, sometimes shockingly so. Skin color was another difference. While skin color was the passport into these neighborhoods, where blacks had moved from the rural South, it was for many a one-way trip. From 1950 to 1966, as U.S. agriculture mechanized, over 5.5 million dislocated black farm workers had moved to the cities, bringing with them, according to Harold Fleming of the Southern Regional Council, the "largest accumulation of social deficits ever visited upon an identifiable group." And once they were there, these new arrivals found their communities surrounded by an invisible fence, as Johnson put it, of "white hatred, prejudice, distaste or condescension" that would prove extremely difficult to negotiate. Individual success stories seemed only to prove the rule. In other words, the war on black poverty, Johnson made clear, would require different strategies and tactics than the war on white poverty, given the very different historical experience, one defined by slavery and segregation, of many blacks in America.

Johnson was unequivocal in his commitment to social change. He declared in truly revolutionary language that achieving real equality for blacks was the "next and the more profound stage of the battle for civil rights. We seek not just freedom but opportunity. We seek not just legal equity but human ability, not just equality as a right and a theory but equality as a fact and equality as a result." This was a striking call for nothing short of a government-directed social revolution, a rare thing in American history. And while many sympathized with the ends, racial justice, others found the means, a greatly empowered federal government, troublesome, fearing the potential for abuse and eventual tyranny. The road to hell, as everyone knows, is surely paved with good intentions.

Like most liberals at this time, Johnson believed in the power of environment to shape and mold people. Public spending to improve life in America's ghettos — such as job training, medical care, public assistance, and education programs — would, it was believed, eventually reduce poverty and thereby bring about the conditions necessary to realize black equality. But Johnson also discussed the role of character, referring to what he thought might be the single most important cause of black poverty: the breakdown of the "Negro family structure," echoing the conclusions of an unpublished report by his assistant secretary of labor, Patrick Moynihan. Moynihan, viewed by some critics as a racist, was a brilliant social scientist (and later U.S. senator, N.Y.) who had observed in 1965 that despite a decrease in black male unemployment, the number of new welfare cases in the black community continued to rise, contradicting expectations and the experience of other groups, and suggesting a link between poverty and single-parent families. As Johnson explained to his audience:

> Only a minority — less than half — of all Negro children reach the age of 18 having lived all their lives with both of their parents. At this moment, tonight, little less than two-thirds are at home with both of their parents. Probably a majority of all Negro children receive federally aided public assistance sometime during their childhood. The family is the cornerstone of our society. More than any other force it shapes the attitude, the hopes, the ambitions, and the values of the child. And when the family collapses, it is the children that are usually damaged. When it happens on a massive scale, the community itself is crippled. So, unless we work to strengthen the family, to create conditions under which most parents will stay together, all the rest — schools, and playgrounds, and public assistance, and private concern — will never be enough to cut completely the circle of despair and deprivation.

It was a remarkable speech that had the potential to unite more conservative Americans, who believed in the importance of a two-parent family, with those who believed that black poverty would be reduced only through an array of well-funded antipoverty programs and, later, by busing and other compulsory means of forcing broader changes in society. LBJ was sadly unable to find common ground on this complex issue as other matters, especially the war in Vietnam, began to press on him. Subsequently, a long, controversial, and tortuous public debate over the connection of family structure to poverty erupted in academe, the press, on campaign trails, in popular culture, and in churches. This debate was complicated by the rise of the women's movement and the introduction of feminist perspectives as well by other points of view drawn from a newly active religious conservatism. In the meantime, black poverty has remained a stubborn fixture of American society. In fact, today 70 percent of black children are born to single mothers. Whatever the cause-and-effect relationship between family structure and poverty, poverty and its many attendant evils has continued to loom large and haunt American inner cities, decades after Johnson put away the speech he gave at Howard University on that promising June day in 1965.

Long ignored, the issues of black freedom and equality captured the imagination and hopes of many Americans in the mid-1960s. It really did appear that the "Negro problem," as it was then called, would finally be addressed. The attention of the country, however, was predictably short-lived as the difficulties and the sheer magnitude of what was involved became apparent. Only a little over 10 percent of the entire population, black numbers were still large enough to affect virtually every institution and to tax the resources of a government trying to address a vast array of other problems, including a cold war abroad and a growing hot war in Vietnam.

But as daunting as the "Negro problem" was, there was more than a little room for optimism. The hard work, constructive effort, and real progress convinced many—it certainly convinced Johnson—that a new era in American race relations was at hand. On signing the voting rights bill into law, on August 6, 1965, Johnson declared,

President Lyndon B. Johnson delivering remarks at the signing ceremony for the Voting Rights Act, 1965. (LBJ Library, WHPO Collection)

Today is a day of triumph for freedom as huge as any victory that has ever been won on any battlefield. Yet to seize the meaning of this day, we must recall darker times. Three and a half centuries ago the first Negroes arrived at Jamestown. They did not arrive in brave ships in search for freedom. They did not mingle fear and joy, in expectation that in this new world anything would be possible to a man strong enough to reach for it. They came in darkness and they came in chains. And today we strike away the last major shackle of those fierce and ancient bonds.

Johnson noted his own role in the history of the civil rights movement by quoting the words he uttered as Senate majority leader in 1957 in support of the civil rights bill of that year: "This right to vote is the basic right without which all others are meaningless. It gives people, people as individuals, control over their own destinies."

Five days after this historic day, a "race riot" broke out, not in the rural South or the urban North but in Watts, a black ghetto in Los Angeles, California — in America's Far West, of all places. The Watts Riot was a six-day rampage started over an incident involving a routine police check. The crowd-turned-mob that gathered, however, would direct most of its fury at area businesses, burning or damaging some six hundred buildings. Shockingly, over thirty lives were lost and over a thousand people injured before order was finally restored. Johnson could not believe the reports coming in from California. He was baffled, as were many who watched their televisions and read their newspapers. "How is it possible," he asked, "after all we've accomplished? How could it be? Is the world topsy-turvy?" The world was indeed. In fact, the Watts Riot was only the beginning of years of madness. More race riots broke out during the long hot summers of 1966, 1967, and 1968, affecting numerous Americans cities, most notably Detroit, New Haven, and Newark. Incredibly, the country experienced five years of urban rioting and looting, if the 1964 race riots in New Jersey, New York, and Illinois are included. A vast and strangely sympathetic literature sprang into being explaining, even justifying, this senseless and wanton destruction. Nevertheless, Johnson's initial baffled reaction to the Watt's Riot got at the truth of the matter: the riots were simply irrational and counterproductive. Moreover, the riots called liberal expectations into serious question, convincing many that what the country really needed was a hardline law-and-order approach.

Reducing black poverty was going to be a major challenge no matter what, but the ghetto riots that plagued Johnson's presidential tenure left the black community in immeasurably worse shape than it had been before. The future of any community lay, of course, in economic development, a combination of individual and cooperative effort. Government programs could help but would never be a substitute for the most important thing in the world—a good paycheck. Martin Luther King, Jr., put the facts of the matter this way in a speech he gave on October 26, 1967, at Philadelphia's Barrett Middle School: "Our slogan must not be, 'Burn, Baby, Burn.' It must be 'Build, Baby, Build.' 'Organize, Baby, Organize.' Yes, our slogan must be 'Learn, Baby, Learn,' so that we can 'Earn, Baby, Earn.'" The work ethic and traditional capitalism, in other words, not self-incineration, were the tested and true ways up and out.

King was murdered by a white racist on April 4, 1968, shot on a balcony outside a Memphis motel room, and despite his lifetime call for nonviolence, there were even more ghetto riots and violence across America that summer. The effect of these years of anarchy and rage was predictable: business investment, such as it was, dried up, and jobs were driven out of the very communities that so desperately needed them. In some riot-torn areas, investment had been chased away apparently for good, as some blocks remain gutted and abandoned to this day. The riots also helped accelerate the migration of white Americans from areas adjacent to, or near, inner cities to the quite refuge and safety of the suburbs, leaving behind boarded-up ghost towns. This population movement from city to suburb, and from the eastern to the western United States, was already well under way for different reasons, but the urban riots and changing housing occupancy patterns in the central city during and after the Johnson years helped turn these population movements into a relative stampede. The alienation and despair of the black community, as bad as it was in 1965, became even worse by the time Johnson left office early in 1969.

The riots occurred at the precise moment when a real breakthrough seemed possible in American race relations. To understand what had gone terribly wrong, Johnson, in July 1967, appointed the National Advisory Commission on Civil Disorders, headed by the governor of Illinois, Ottis Kerner, Jr. The Kerner, or Riot, Commission issued the famous but meaningless warning: "Our nation is moving toward two societies, one black, one white — separate and unequal." The warning was empty because the country was not "moving" toward two societies at all (although more blacks were physically moving to the ghetto); it was already a nation of two societies, in terms of blacks and whites, and had been for decades. Integrating the much smaller black society into the country's mainstream was, after all, the entire point of the early civil rights movement, which had just achieved its biggest successes with the 1964 and 1965 civil rights acts. The Great Society programs were designed, in part, to help transition the country to life in postsegregation America. The riots themselves, the Kerner Commission concluded, were due to black frustration at the lack of economic opportunity. The impatience with the rate of progress left liberal Americans urging the government to step up its antipoverty programs, create more jobs, and act more aggressively to end racial discrimination.

Despite the Watts Riot, the American West was not a region in which race had figured very large in the American imagination, except, of course, in terms of "cowboys and Indians" — a Hollywood caricature of western history that left little room for the region's underlying multiracial complexity. During the postwar era, the relationship between the U.S. government and Indian country changed abruptly. The federal policy of termination emphasized assimilation, on the one hand, and the rapid phasing out of the government's commitments to and programs for Native Americans, on the other. Termination had

been adopted in reaction to Franklin Roosevelt's policy of plu-
ralism and effort to stop, even reverse, allotment, and was given
urgency with the onset of the global struggle against a new "red
menace." Tribal ownership of land, and the reservation system
in general, as well as collective values struck some as a little too
much like communism and, in the middle of the Cold War, as
too un-American, the ironies notwithstanding. It would be
hard to explain to a Martian why white America had a long
history of trying to integrate Native Americans in the nation's
life and an equally long history of successfully excluding African
Americans from the same; of wanting to dismantle the Indian
reservations, which were seen as temporary, but of wanting to
maintain black communities on a segregated and permanent
basis.

By the time Kennedy came to office and the reform-minded
Stuart Udall took over the Department of the Interior, support
for termination had collapsed, and a search for a middle ground
ensued. On March 6, 1968, Johnson delivered a special message
to Congress, "The Forgotten American," which dealt exclusively
with Indian affairs, announcing a new, really a blended, federal
policy. Johnson stressed Indian self-help and self-respect, which
reassured conservatives, and the continuation, indeed expansion, of U.S. assistance, which won over liberals. Combining
self-determination and federal support proved to be a successful
political formula, a synthesis, really, of decades of federal policy.
It proved consequential and essentially defines U.S.–Indian relations to this day.

Hispanic Americans, even though they were destined to be
the largest minority group in the United States by the beginning of the twenty-first century, were, like Native Americans,
largely ignored. This changed when César Chávez, a Mexican
American leader from Yuma, Arizona, along with the United
Farm Workers, a labor union he helped found, launched a boy-
cott of table grapes in 1965 that lasted for five years, a tactic that
was ultimately successful in forcing the growers to bend to the
union's demands.

The federal government had dammed the waters of the West,

a massive tax-supported boon, which had brought a wealthy and oligarchic class of growers into existence. The early supporters of reclamation were much more democratic in their intentions, however, believing a regional system of dams, reservoirs, and canals would put in place a hydraulic infrastructure that would enable a new Jeffersonian yeomanry to flourish and prosper in the western states and create a cheap and abundant energy source. No one early in the twentieth century (the Newlands Reclamation Act was passed in 1902) had signed on for creating a small number of growers dependent on exploiting thousands of landless workers, but that is exactly what the West got. Washington and the state capitals, from Austin to Sacramento, chose to ignore the plight of this new underclass of agricultural workers, many migratory and desperately poor, whose lot was brought to national attention as early as 1939 with the publications of John Steinbeck's novel *The Grapes of Wrath*, and Carey McWilliams's nonfictional work *Factories in the Field*.

What is more, border enforcement was neglected, allowing illegal or undocumented workers from Mexico to enter the country easily. This ever-ready and seemingly endless supply of cheap labor kept wages down, working conditions poor, union organization in the United States weak, and the modernization of the economy in Mexico on hold. A porous border worked against the interests of U.S. workers, organized and otherwise, but certainly offered the growers more government help, if indirect help, with their bottom line. But what was much more important, from the standpoint of what is the greatest good for the greatest number, these utilitarian policies of benign neglect kept the nation's food bill very low, which benefited all Americans — rich and poor alike.

The progress that was made on civil rights was due in no small part to the talent and abilities of some extraordinary leaders — Lyndon Johnson, Martin Luther King, Jr., and César Chávez. As different as these men were in their style and goals, they all had one thing in common: they each possessed a national vision and had a real program of reform. Essentially, these men were Americans first, reformers second. But the problems that followed segregation, including "white backlash," helped produce decidedly "second rate" leaders in the late 1960s, in Johnson's apt generalization, each of whom promoted a narrow racial or ethnic chauvinism. In 1966, Johnson stated, "Americans are rightly concerned about the civil disorders that have taken place in some of our cities. The leaders of those disorders are just as bigoted in their own way as those who now seek to exploit 'white backlash.' It is our public duty to prosecute them when they endanger the lives and property of innocent people—negro or white."

One such opportunist was George Wallace, a white racist and governor of Alabama. In his inaugural speech (given in 1963), Wallace taunted the country with the words "I draw the line in the dust and toss the gauntlet before the feet of tyranny, and I say segregation now, segregation tomorrow, segregation forever." He appealed to white workers in both the North and the South who had become disaffected with the Democratic Party and its strong position on civil rights. On the other side of the racial divide, the Black Muslim and separatist Malcolm X had threatened, "Our objective is complete freedom, justice and equality *by any means necessary*" (he was assassinated in 1965). And there were the needlessly confrontational leaders of the Black Panthers, Bobby Seale and Huey Newton. Eldridge Cleaver, another Black Panther, author of *Soul on Ice* (1968) and hero of the radical left, infamously described his raping of white women, after he first practiced on black women, as "an insurrectionary act."

Some Hispanic Americans, and later Native Americans, were infected with a similar racial or ethnic militancy. In Colorado, Rudolfo "Corky" Gonzales called for a Chicano self-determination; in northern New Mexico, Reies López Tijerina demanded an investigation into the legal disposition, by avaricious Anglo attorneys, of the old land grants, a process that dated back to the end of the Mexican War. And he tried to found the Republic of San Joaquín del Río Chama. And in Texas, José Ángel Gutiérrez helped found the Mexican American Youth Organization in

1967 and later the Raza Unida Party, which promoted a Chicano nationalism — a spiritual return to Aztlán. This mythical place, another City of Cíbola, was an irredentist belief in a northern Aztec homeland, connecting the Chicano movement with a heroic past. The American Indian Movement was founded in 1968 by young Indian leaders, such as Dennis Banks and Russell Means, who wanted to draw attention to Indian issues and problems by staging highly symbolic protests. For example, in 1971 the group occupied Mount Rushmore, a federal site on former Indian land. Much of the 1960s was indeed forward looking, even futuristic minded. But Wallace, Malcolm X, Tijerina, and the rest of the many racial and ethnic chauvinists of this period seemed like a throwback to the romantic nationalism of the nineteenth century, a deeply troubled period in European history. Fortunately, relatively little civil violence came out of all of this speechmaking and posturing.

What all of these atavists shared was a primitive tribalism. That they were able to attract any followers at all certainly says something about the troubled and emotional times when Johnson was president. The sense that the country was moving in the wrong direction was growing, and the strong popular support that Johnson had enjoyed in 1964, as measured by public opinion polls, had fallen sharply four years later — a decline caused by many factors, without a doubt the most important of which was the military situation in Vietnam. The war poisoned public discourse, and like a vial of black ink poured into a bowl of water, it spread throughout and poisoned much of Johnson's presidency. Things became so toxic, in fact, that Johnson announced in 1968 that he would not seek a second term — a decision that was a good one perhaps for Johnson's own peace of mind but a tragedy for the country.

It is difficult to judge Johnson and this period in American race relations because there are no other cases with which to compare it. No other advanced industrialized democracy has ever attempted to integrate a minority so distinctly set apart from the majority by race, culture, and history, as were African Americans. South Africa comes closest to mind. But the differences between South Africa, where power was in the hands of a minority, and the United States really outweigh any similarity. The U.S. situation was simply unique. And what is astonishing is how much Johnson accomplished, given how unexpectedly turbulent postsegregation proved to be. There was the growing disaffection of conservative white Southerners from the Democratic Party, on the one hand, and the political opposition from the left, from members of Johnson's own party, on the other. The Left's noisy and militant protests (everybody seemed to be yelling at each other) were mostly directed at the war, but they nevertheless hampered Johnson's ability to do other things, things with which the Left was in accord. But this was definitely a throw-the-baby-out-with-the-bathwater crowd. Still, Johnson's impressive record on civil rights, the passage of the civil rights acts of 1964, 1965, and 1968, is comparable to only one other president in U.S. history, Abraham Lincoln. In fact, there is an overwhelming consensus among American blacks and whites that the gains of the civil rights movement were real. And as stubborn as black poverty has proved to be, there is also a thriving and culturally assimilated black middle class, which continues to grow in size and wealth.

While black poverty was many things, it was not invisible. Indeed, black poverty was painfully evident in almost every large city where a black community existed, where it was invariably located in the "poorest part of town." Michael Harrington, a St. Louis socialist and acute observer of American society, discovered the existence of another kind of poverty, however, one far less visible and no more acceptable in a booming postwar economy: a society rich in private goods yet poor in public services, as economist John Kenneth Galbraith also noted in his widely read *The Affluent Society* (1958). Reformers never tired of reminding their fellow Americans that poverty in the midst of so much plenty was intolerable — a compelling moral argument. It was originally framed in national terms but has since been globalized, with the contrast now drawn between the world's rich nations and desperately poor regions, such as sub-Saharan Africa.

Harrington's short book *The Other America*, published in 1962, well after the start of the civil rights movement, electrified the Kennedy administration. In response, it launched an anti-poverty campaign headed by Sargent Shriver. As president, LBJ would widen this campaign into a "war." Ending black poverty was certainly one of Johnson's goals, but this was only one front, and blacks were a minority of the country's poor, which Harrington, using government statistics, reckoned to be between 40 and 50 million citizens. These included, he wrote, "the unskilled workers, the migrant farm workers, the aged, the minorities, and all the others who live in the economic underworld of American life." This was a poverty that went far beyond the black ghetto, was white and brown as well as black, male as well as female, affected children as well as the aged, and reached from coast to coast. The only minority Harrington overlooked, which he later regretted, for they were the "poorest of all," was the American Indian — the true invisible man. The nation's poverty did not exist in isolated pockets, Harrington argued, as much as it was distributed throughout as well as in the "interstices" of society. To abolish this largely "invisible" poverty, it first had to be defined. And after study, the government in 1964 did just that: the official poverty line was drawn at a family income of less than $3,000. Still, this was the easy part. Ending poverty itself would be much, much harder, for in addition to being invisible, it was also rooted, Harrington trenchantly observed, in a culture, or subculture, of misery that tended to be self-perpetuating. Bad decisions tended to lead to more bad decisions.

On April 24, 1964, Johnson declared war on poverty on the front porch of a shack in Inez, Kentucky, in the midst of Appalachia, a region of the country synonymous with poverty, cultural backwardness, and few good-paying jobs outside the coal mines — with their black lung and terrifying cave-ins, where men were entombed alive. As Johnson intoned (Lady Bird by his side), "The Appalachians Ranges were the first challenge and the first test to the settlers of this seaboard. Through the Cumberland Gap Americans found their way to the promise

Lyndon B. Johnson in the Oval Office with press secretary George
Reedy in background, 1964. (LBJ Library, WHPO Collection)

and the plenty of a continent that is united. It is not too much to suggest that today we may again find our way to new promise and new fulfillment by taking up the human challenge of modern Appalachia." This War on Poverty was the core of his Great Society, and it was staggering in its ambition, cost, degree of difficulty, and planning — lots of planning, which alarmed conservatives, fearful of a controlling state.

Ambition LBJ had always possessed in plenty, a quality not unique to political leaders, but certainly his personal ambition was extraordinary, and his ambition for his country was no less so. And LBJ had vision, having learned to think in terms of broad, national purpose in FDR's Washington. In this respect, he was very much a product of his time, when leaders still dreamed of winning broad majorities and assembling new coalitions so that they could undertake bold and great things: defeating fear and restoring confidence in the country's institutions, taking on totalitarianism, standing up against the communist world, lifting up the world's poor, rebuilding entire cities anew through slum clearance and new housing projects, constructing vast new transportation systems, putting a man on the moon, wiping out disease and hunger, enlarging democracy's foundations, educating every citizen, erecting monumental works of public art, promoting the arts and humanities, restoring the environment, and eliminating poverty at home. Dreaming big was a habit of mind, and an expensive one, that distinguished the 1960s. It certainly distinguished LBJ.

And creating a society free of want is a hard thing. The very daring of it, like putting a man on the moon, is breathtaking in its sheer audacity. The War on Poverty, in short, was not a slogan but an undertaking that was intended to be achieved. To win this war, Johnson passed a number of programs to feed the poor, nurse the sick, and take care of the elderly. The food stamp program, a revival of an older program, did help feed the poor; Medicare (funded and administered by the federal government) did help the elderly pay their medical bills; and Medicaid (funded by the states and the federal government but administered by the states) did provide medical care for the

President Lyndon B. Johnson visits with Job Corps students at Camp Gary Job Corps Center, 1965. (LBJ Library; WHPO Collection)

poor. Medicare and Medicaid, like so many of Johnson's social welfare measures, were both passed in 1965 by the industrious and progressive-minded Eighty-Ninth Congress. While these two programs fell far short of a real national health care system, the last great agenda item of American liberalism, they still helped millions of Americans, including the elderly, afford to visit a doctor and obtain needed medicines and care.

Whether the Great Society reduced poverty remains an open question, although poverty did decline during Johnson's presidency. Whether it was a result of his myriad programs or the low unemployment (in addition to a strong economy, there was also a war going on) of this period, the social efficacy of the Great Society remains as much an academic as a political question. What does appear to be true — a rather unremarkable fact at that — is that if one compares social spending under Democratic and Republican administrations from 1960 right into the twenty-first century, there is a clear correlation between increased spending on antipoverty programs and the decline in poverty itself.

Much of Johnson's Great Society, as the expression itself denotes, was about people — about how people were to relate to each other, despite differences in class or race. Gender would increasingly become an issue, fueled as it was by a new women's movement, itself based on postwar affluence, inspired by the civil rights and antiwar movements (the National Organization of Women was founded in 1966), and set against the social backdrop of the baby boom and a sexual revolution in morality and behavior. Antibiotics essentially eliminated the threat of traditional venereal diseases, such as syphilis and gonorrhea, and improvements in contraception, notably the advent of the birth control pill in 1960, gave women, in theory at least, real control over their own biology. However, the effects of this liberalization and the significant expansion of individual freedom it represented — in social, political, legal, economic, and cultural terms — were not fully felt until the following decade. The 1970s were years when an opposite but probably not an equal reaction occurred to these changes in the lives of women, one that St. Louis's Phyllis Schlafly and many others would use to energize the country's dormant conservative base to start a movement to counter feminism and champion family values.

Unlike the women's movement, which to be sure was becoming a major force in American life during the 1960s (Betty Friedan's nerve-hitting *Feminine Mystique* was published in 1963, the same year Johnson became president), the environmental movement was already well under way by the 1960s. In fact, the Wilderness Act, the culmination of years of work by Howard Zahnhiser, Wallace Stegner, and many others, was approved by Johnson in 1964. As he eloquently put it, "If future generations are to remember us with gratitude rather than contempt, we must leave them more than the miracles of technology. We must leave them a glimpse of the world as it was in the beginning, not just after we got through with it."

It was the landmark work of a woman, however, a marine biologist named Rachel Carson, that would change a movement defined by conservationist and preservationist concerns, dating back to the nineteenth century, into something more sophisticated but also unfortunate and counterproductive in many ways. This change occurred during Johnson's years as president. Carson's *Silent Spring* (1962) raised the prospect that use of pesticides could do great damage to nature and to humans themselves by introducing chemicals into the great chain of being. This was an altogether different kind of matter than saving a canyon, forest, or vulnerable species. Carson argued, and brilliantly so, that the chemical industry threatened not just a special place or creature but life itself. Nature, according to Carson, was not something that existed beyond the backyard fence, past city limits, or as a place one physically went to, as if to an island refuge. Rather it was found everywhere there was life, indeed inside one's very own body. Synthetic chemicals could become lodged in our very tissues, proof, if any more proof were needed, that all living things were connected. The reaction to this persuasive book, as to other consciousness-raising books in American history, such as Upton Sinclair's *The Jungle* (1906), was a call for reform of the chemical industry, just as Sinclair's book called for reform of the meatpacking industry. Johnson's Great Society would continue to answer the call, addressing the general abuses of industry against nature, an effort started under Kennedy and that would culminate under Nixon and Ford.

Thus, Johnson signed legislation rooted in the older values of aesthetics, recreation, preservation, and conservation. These laws included the Land and Water Conservation Act of 1965, Solid Waste Disposal Act of 1965, Motor Vehicle Air Pollution Control Act of 1965, National Historic Preservation Act of 1966, Endangered Species Preservation Act of 1966, National Trails System Act of 1968, Wild and Scenic Rivers Act of 1968, and Aircraft Noise Abatement Act of 1968. However, the ground was set during his term for the more comprehensive National Environmental Policy Act of 1969 and the creation of the Environmental Protection Agency in 1970. As constructive, even necessary, as these many measures were, they were not dependent on sentiment and nostalgia alone but drew on a scientifically informed environmentalism. Carson's clarion call derived its power from science, but it helped inspire an antiscientific environmentalism that took her work as a withering critique on progress as well as on science and technology itself. Those who came to view the military-industrial complex as run by a heartless technocracy, and fueled by the almost inhuman ambitions of power mongers like LBJ, found fertile ground for their paranoia in Carson's *Silent Spring*. The New Deal, which was designed to replace an out-of-whack capitalism that benefited only a few with an economy managed instead to support a growing middle class had now become the new Leviathan, with Johnson riding astride its mighty back, that had to be stopped. In this odd way, the freedom of Goldwater Republicans and the freedom espoused by the war protesters and those who made up the counterculture, from the urban hippies to the rural communes, appeared not dissimilar. If Johnson could be reviled by both the Left and the Right, then even the most adroit politician could be overtaken by events, especially if those events had as their sordid backdrop an incomprehensible and distant war. Like the conquistadors of old, LBJ boldly sallied forth to once again find the Seven Cities of Cíbola. What he found instead was Saigon, a harsh reality very far away from his dreams.

In 1959, North Vietnam fatefully chose to embark on a high-risk strategy of actively supporting a communist takeover of South Vietnam and to start a drive to reunify the country, despite the United States' public commitment five years before to protect South Vietnam. Not willing initially to take on the United States directly, the North, through the Viet Cong insurgents in South Vietnam, confined itself to a low-intensity conflict — political murders, bombings, raids — violence that began to consume, like a gnawing cancer, life below the seventeenth parallel. In response to the growing violence, Kennedy sent in thousands of U.S. military advisors to assist with South Vietnam's counterinsurgency, an effort complicated by the difficulties of fighting an enemy that had the advantage of a shared border. Thus, North Vietnam and the United States were engaged in a bloody proxy war in South Vietnam.

The turning point came with the military coup and cold-blooded execution of Ngo Dinh Diem on November 2, 1963, three weeks before Kennedy's assassination in Dallas. The situation in South Vietnam was already tense with the Buddhist crisis — saffron-robbed monks angry at Diem's favoritism of the country's Catholic minority. Now, without Diem's strong leadership and fierce anticommunism, both of which probably outweighed his political provocations and nepotism, the likelihood of a communist takeover in the South became a real possibility. The communists, after all, were exceptionally well organized, highly motivated, bankrolled, and willing to kill and take very heavy casualties. There was no substitute for total victory; the conflict was neither politics nor business. For the North, it was war.

The existence of North Vietnam's "deliberate and systematic campaign of aggression" in the South was not formally acknowledged by the U.S. Congress until it passed the Gulf of Tonkin Resolution in 1964, its response to a minor naval engagement in which the North Vietnamese, on August 2, opened fire on the USS *Maddox* in the South China Sea (a second attack was believed to have occurred two days later but now appears to have been entirely the product of "skewed" intelligence). Real or imagined, the crisis in the Gulf of Tonkin raised the issue of freedom of the seas, which resonated in a maritime nation that had explicitly fought two wars to preserve it, the War of 1812 and the First World War. Thus, the political significance of the Gulf of Tonkin incident transcended Cold War politics, even as it made absolutely no sense except within a Cold War context. At bottom, the incident was a consequence of the rising military tensions — by sea, on land, and in the air — between the Democratic Republic of Vietnam, the United States, and their respective proxies.

On August 7, 1964, Congress declared that the "United States regards as vital to its national interests and to world peace the maintenance of international peace and security in southeast Asia . . . [and] is, therefore, prepared, as the President determines, to take all necessary steps, including the use of armed force, to assist [South Vietnam] in defense of its freedom." The terms of this joint resolution were as sweeping as its passage was nearly unanimous: the vote for it in the House of Representatives was 416 to 0; in the U.S. Senate, 88 to 2. Only two western politicians, Wayne Morse of Oregon and Ernest Gruening of Alaska, cast votes in opposition. In Johnson's political, albeit earthy, judgment, the resolution was "like Grandma's nightshirt. It covered everything." Congress intended to give whoever won the presidency that fall, Johnson or Goldwater, a free hand to deal with the situation in Southeast Asia. Johnson won by a landslide but did not decide to take war directly to the North until February 7, 1965, following a deadly mortar attack by the Viet Cong on the U.S. airbase in Pleiku. His two other options were to continue waging a limited proxy war, Kennedy-style, in the South, which had produced nothing but frustration, or to leave the South to the North, thereby conceding communism a victory, however small in the grand scheme of things, but one for which he and his party would no

President Lyndon B. Johnson meeting with the Joint Chiefs of Staff at the LBJ Ranch, 1964. Clockwise from LBJ: Secretary of Defense Robert McNamara, Major General Chester Clifton, General Curtis LeMay, General Earle Wheeler, Deputy Secretary of Defense Cyrus Vance, General Harold Johnson, Admiral David McDonald, and General Wallace Greene. (LBJ Library, WHPO Collection)

doubt have paid a heavy political price. In the end, Johnson made good on his slain predecessor's inaugural warning: "Let every nation know, whether it wishes us well or ill, that we shall pay any price, bear any burden, meet any hardship, support any friend, oppose any foe, in order to assure the survival and the success of liberty." Johnson ordered Operation Rolling Thunder, a bombing campaign conducted by the U.S. Air Force (using aircraft such as the F-4 Phantom, the F-105 Thunderchief, and the F-100 Super Saber) to punish Hanoi and shore up the weak government in Saigon. Johnson made clear that failure in Vietnam, or anywhere else, was not an option.

Thousands of things have been written about Vietnam. In

the end, the United States expended blood and treasure out of cold logic rather than because of calculations based on its own history and vital interests. Communists were the enemy, and the North Vietnamese were communists. Therefore, the United States went to war with North Vietnam. Johnson's decision to take the fight to the North was thus perfectly rational, even syllogistic, and intellectually defensible as such. But it meant falling into the illogic of trying to defend a country that would not or could not defend itself, unless the United States was prepared to remain in South Vietnam indefinitely. To the North, who saw the world through a very crude Marxist prism, the relationship of the United States to South Vietnam was essentially imperialistic. It was no longer 1898, of course, but the harder the United States fought to defend South Vietnam, the more it seemed to make the communist case, at least in the communist world, for American colonialism.

Answering this charge, Johnson, at Johns Hopkins University on April 7, 1965, shortly after having escalated the ground and air war, explained the U.S. position about as clearly as the English language permits: "Vietnam is far away from this quiet campus. We have no territory there, nor do we seek any. . . . Our objective is the independence of South Vietnam, and its freedom from attack. We want nothing for ourselves — only that the people of South Vietnam be allowed to guide their own country in their own way." But Johnson went beyond a statement of the obvious in terms of U.S. intentions. In the same address, he pointed out an equally obvious fact that "these countries of southeast Asia are home for millions of impoverished people." And Johnson held out a remarkable offer. He declared that there "must be a much more massive effort to improve the life of man in that conflict-torn corner of our world." He then laid out a generous program of development — "The first step is for the countries of southeast Asia to associate themselves in a greatly expanded cooperative effort for development" — and added that "we would hope that North Vietnam would take its place in the common effort just as soon as peaceful cooperation is possible."

He noted that the "United Nations is already actively engaged in development in this area"; however,

> for our part I will ask the Congress to join in a billion dollar American investment in this effort. . . . And I would hope that all other industrialized countries, including the Soviet Union, will join in this effort to replace despair with hope, and terror with progress. The task is nothing less than to enrich the hopes and the existence of more than a hundred million people. And there is much to be done. The vast Mekong River can provide food and water and power on a scale to dwarf even our own TVA. The wonders of modern medicine can be spread through villages where thousands die every year from lack of care. Schools can be established to train people in the skills that are needed to manage the process of development. . . . I also intend to expand and speed up a program to make available our farm surpluses to assist in feeding and clothing the needy in Asia. We should not allow people to go hungry and wear rags while our own warehouses overflow with an abundance of wheat and corn, rice and cotton.

In short, Johnson was proposing a New Deal for Southeast Asia, directed and financed by the United States, to be sure, but a program that involved real aid to nations in real need. Surely, the people's revolution could be put on hold while Vietnam and neighboring countries modernized and raised their standards of living, with the help and assistance from the international community. Proponents of the alternative were trying to offer the hope that a poor agricultural economy could somehow collectivize its way to industrialization. The problem was that the leaders of the people's revolution, with their Marxist blinders firmly in place, rejected any U.S. role if it meant a divided Vietnam. So instead of dotting the Vietnam countryside with dams, roads, schools, and hospitals, financed with foreign capital, local energy was diverted into building overland supply trails and underground staging areas, such as Cu Chi tunnels, as well as other militarily impressive but economically worthless projects. The North rejected Johnson's bunch of carrots; the communists insisted that Vietnam's power should be concentrated in the dreary, ochre-colored administrative buildings of Hanoi, and not shared with a South having strong economic and political links to the free market and democratic world. The only thing that can be said is that if Johnson's offer had been accepted by the North, Vietnam as a whole would have been immeasurably better off. But since this road was not taken, Johnson was left with nothing but a very big stick with which to try to change the hearts and minds of the Vietnamese, in the North and in the South. Given human nature to resist coercion, this was a very dubious prospect indeed, as subsequent events tragically showed.

Thus was Johnson's dilemma. The liberal justification for U.S. power was that it exists to do good. Since the North rejected American plans to develop the South and integrate Indochina into the capitalist economy, this meant that Johnson, if he were going to stop the North's plans to unify the country and integrate Vietnam into the communist trading block, had to wage war against the very people he purported to help. No matter how much Johnson's position could be argued to have made sense in the broader abstract terms of geopolitics, the contradiction at the local level could not be reconciled; the violent means simply did not seem to square with the peaceful ends. And the harder Johnson tried — the more targets he ordered bombed, the more ground troops he committed — the more he appeared to be the very thing he denied: a foreign interloper, and a bully at that. And as the United States was using its awesome firepower to pulverize a poor, backward country, the question of what was good became more muddled even as it became more urgent. It became increasingly clear as 1965 turned into 1966, 1966 turned into 1967, and 1967 turned into 1968 that if the United States had not taken charge of the military situation — and at one point there were more than half a million troops stationed in South Vietnam — the South, notwithstanding Washington's serious efforts at nation-building (to this day, the difference in the level of development between

President Lyndon B. Johnson addressing a crowd of Vietnam War supporters in Indianapolis, 1966. (LBJ Library, WHPO Collection)

Hanoi and Saigon remains so striking that it can produce a sense of culture shock) would have fallen, leaving America's ally to the mercy of the North.

Johnson's predicament in Southeast Asia has often been likened to a man stuck in a quagmire: the more the man struggled to extricate himself, the more he became mired in it. Not everyone fully grasped the nature of Johnson's predicament, including Johnson himself, at least not at first. Nevertheless, he had to make the case to the American people for "why we must take this painful road." Conscription, paradoxically, made the president's case for war more difficult to make, not less. For conscription to be accepted in a democracy, it must imply a broader consent. Absent consent, and in the United States this means bipartisan consent, conscription itself, rather than foreign policy, becomes the issue, raising as it does old and legitimate concerns about "the rights of Englishmen" and fears of standing armies. True, Johnson had, by virtue of the Gulf of Tonkin Resolution, the Congressional authority to take any military action he deemed necessary, short of starting another war with China, as had happened in Korea in an earlier and remarkably parallel situation.

Indeed, the lessons of the Korean War — political, military, and otherwise — were very much on Johnson's mind as he sought to avoid ruining his presidency, as Truman had done his, by fighting yet another unpopular war in Asia. On the other hand, the Korean settlement, ultimately reached by Eisenhower in 1953, provided ample evidence that if the United States stuck to its guns, South Vietnam, like South Korea before it, might very well be saved from the communists. The hard-won success in Korea, in fact, assured that any president, Democratic or Republican, would make a serious effort to contain communism in Vietnam: what was good for the Korean goose would no doubt be equally good for the Vietnamese gander. And Johnson enjoyed Congress's explicit support to take military action in Vietnam, unlike Truman, who acted on his own authority and U.N. sanction to defend South Korea.

But the United States had changed since 1953. A new generation had grown up — the baby boomers — and it fell to Johnson to try to convince the young men in this cohort to fight and possibly die in a poor land ten thousand miles away from home. This would have been a hard sell at any time, but especially so in 1965, when America, in Johnson's words, was "bursting with opportunity and promise," thereby making going off to war especially hard to do. And there had been no spectacular provocation, after all, such as the Japanese's pugnacious attack on Pearl Harbor. Whatever the facts of the Gulf of Tonkin incident (some critics charged that Johnson exaggerated the nature of the attacks), it was not Pearl Harbor. Thus, there was no particular sense of urgency, except for the immediate concern about the short-term viability and sustaining power of the government in Saigon. U.S. strategic interests in the Pacific were arguably not at stake, as events subsequent to 1975, when the United States entirely withdrew from the country, were to prove, and the U.S. Seventh Fleet faced little threat from the North Vietnamese navy. U.S. bases in the Philippines (Clark Air Base and Subic Bay Naval Base) were all but immune from attack from Southeast Asia. America's position in this corner of the globe would have perhaps been complicated by the loss of South Vietnam but not fundamentally compromised. Commercial shipping would obviously have continued unvexed through the Strait of Molucca and other nearby sea lanes. So worries about the possible impact of the loss of this free market on the world economy were indeed minimal.

Of far greater moment was the breaking of America's word to a struggling ally, its international commitments, and other Cold War considerations — not least of which were the lessons of the Munich Agreement, the result of a 1938 conference between Great Britain and France and the fascist powers of Germany and Italy. Munich was constantly invoked in the postwar era, shorthand for expressing the need to stand up to dictators, whether of the *volk* or the proletariat, lest Western inaction — or worse, appeasement — be construed as weakness and an invitation to further aggression. In a world of nuclear weapons, America and the West could not afford to indulge in the pacifist fantasies of Great Britain's interwar prime minister, Neville Chamberlain, and by analogy surrender South Vietnam to communism, as Chamberlain and Édouard Daladier had once surrendered the Sudetenland to fascism.

There was considerable weight to all these arguments for taking the war directly to the North Vietnamese — to expand a localized war and take it in an entirely new direction in order to cut off, isolate, and kill the counterinsurgents in South Vietnam. Johnson's decision to escalate the war was bold. It was also a huge risk — as all wars are a risk — to American lives, treasure, and prestige. A great many young men responded to the challenge, believed in the cause, enlisted or were inducted, served honorably and courageously, and after their terms of service expired, went on to contribute to society in many positive ways.

But many other good men came to question the war and the need to make such sacrifices. These doubts were reinforced when, after four very long years, the war failed to produce the promised results, a point that was driven home early in 1968, when the enemy was still able to launch an impressive offensive, which took the fighting to Saigon and other cities, forcing a major reassessment of America's military prospects. Walter Cronkite, a highly regarded news reporter, observed on February 27, 1968, in the offensive's aftermath, "To say that we are mired in stalemate seems the only realistic, yet unsatisfactory, conclusion . . . it is increasingly clear to this reporter that the only rational way out then will be to negotiate, not as victors, but as an honorable people who lived up to their pledge to defend democracy, and did the best they could."

In the meantime, the questioning by draftees or those likely to be drafted led to an ethical and moral dilemma as old as Plato's dialogues; namely, is the citizen of the state obliged to obey the laws with which he disagrees? There is no easy answer to this question, the clarity of Socrates' own logic notwithstanding, and it divided many a conscience, family, and ultimately society itself — a society that was already unsettled by the civil rights movement, which called into question the laws segregating the races and which had advocated civil disobedience as one remedy. To many on the far left, or what was called the New Left, injustice at home mirrored injustice abroad, and not a few saw the two evils as originating from a common source. These radicals looked to Mao Zedong, Ho Chi Minh, Fidel Castro, and Che Guevara, whose experience could not have been less relevant to modern America, for ideological inspiration. The result was revolutionary prescriptions that were hopelessly, even ridiculously, at odds with U.S. political and social realities. Whether antiwar protestors had heard of the Port Huron Statement, Students for a Democratic Society, or the New Left, many bought into a general critique of U.S. involvement in Vietnam for the plain reason that, at bottom, they did not want to risk life and limb in an unpopular war. Once Nixon ended the draft in 1973, but not the military presence of the United States around the world, the antiwar movement declined sharply, revealing starkly that basic self-preservation, not ideology, was the antiwar movement's driving force. But during Johnson's presidency, unrest over the war helped set the stage for the Left to turn on itself, which it did with abandon, destroying the Democratic majority that had held together since FDR.

The United States, as defender of the Western liberal tradition, found itself recast and vilified by the growing antiwar movement, with its cruel chant: "Hey, hey, LBJ, how many kids did you kill today?" In the more fervid imaginations of the street protesters, the United States was just another empire, little different from the Soviet Union, and engaged in doing what empires do: extending its sway in some part of the world, in this case Southeast Asia. If the United States were working to do good, defeating Nazis or Kamikazes, that was one thing. But if to realize its broader purposes in the world, the U.S. government deemed it necessary to put down authentic nationalist movements or genuine revolutionary uprisings, then it was time to burn flags and draft cards. The antiwar movement failed to stop the war; the North Vietnamese army accomplished that. Given the sheer numbers involved and their frequency, antiwar protests did, however, provide comfort to the enemy and thereby helped prolong the war. Pacifism definitely kills, although very few antiwar protesters had the honesty or common sense to admit this fact, believing somehow that only Johnson heard their chants or saw their demonstrations. And while the antiwar movement was ineffectual in changing policy in any way (Johnson and Nixon both ignored them, although they certainly contributed to Johnson's decision not to run for reelection), they were affirming to those participating and had a powerful theatricality and drama. Moreover, the antiwar demonstrations were set against a remarkable soundtrack of protest music, such as "Fortunate Son" (1969), by the California band Creedence Clearwater Revival, which took aim at the rich and privileged who started wars but left the poor everyman to do the fighting, a class-based division of labor Nixon would later institutionalize with the all-volunteer military. "Fortunate Son" was probably the best of this genre, and its angry lyrics pounded out:

> Some folks are born made to wave the flag,
> Ooh, they're red, white and blue.
> And when the band plays hail to the chief,
> Ooh, they point the cannon at you, lord,
>
> It ain't me, it ain't me, I ain't no senator's son, son.
> It ain't me, it ain't me; I ain't no fortunate one, no.
>
> Some folks are born silver spoon in hand,
> Lord, don't they help themselves, oh.
> But when the taxman comes to the door,
> Lord, the house looks like a rummage sale, yes.
>
> It ain't me, it ain't me, I ain't no millionaire's son, no.
> It ain't me, it ain't me; I ain't no fortunate one, no.
>
> Yeah!
> Some folks inherit star spangled eyes,
> Ooh, they send you down to war, lord,
> And when you ask them, how much should we give?
> Ooh, they only answer more! more! more!
>
> It ain't me, it ain't me, I ain't no military son, son.
> It ain't me, it ain't me; I ain't no fortunate one, one.

It ain't me, it ain't me, I ain't no fortunate one, no, no, no,
It ain't me, it ain't me, I ain't no fortunate son, no, no, no.

This song carried a simple class sentiment and sense of justice
that called to mind the music of Woody Guthrie. It needs to be
said, however, that notwithstanding the availability of college
and other deferments, at least the draft attempted to share the
burden of military service widely through society. This was
something Johnson, who saw himself as anything but a "fortunate son," took for granted and implied in many of his public
remarks. But as the face of the establishment, which apparently
sought only power and aggrandizement, he found himself
widely, even contemptuously ignored on the point of shared
sacrifice.

Indeed, it was not the ancient questions posed by the philo-
sophical Greeks that were relevant to pubic discourse in the
mid-1960s, but the cautionary lessons of the corrupt and deca-
dent Roman Empire. And as the war in Vietnam dragged on,
Johnson went from being seen as the leader of the free world to
being regarded as more of a bad Roman emperor, to some a
war-mongering tyrant, who sought to enlarge his power at the
expense of everyone else's liberty—at home and overseas, all
the while pretending, in a Stetson instead of a toga, to honor
the values and institutions of the old republic.

Of course, the United States had its own version of the Roman Republic, and an official nostalgia to go with it: the storied
Old West. Most Americans turned to their cowboys, rather
than to the more aloof Romans, to recall a time when things
were simpler and made more sense; when good always seemed
to triumph over evil. Johnson had proved to be a genius at
exploiting the frontier myth for political ends. There was his
fabled ranch and the potent symbol he had turned it into. But
he also knew how to evoke this heroic age when he called on
U.S. forces to "come home with that coonskin on the wall," or
when he compared Vietnam to Texas: "Just like the Alamo,
somebody damn well needed to go to their aid. Well, by God,
I'm going to Viet Nam's aid!" In fact, as the Left turned on

Johnson, it came to turn on the mythic West as well, equating the expanding frontier and nation building of the nineteenth century with America's *imperium* in the twentieth. The subjugation of Native Americans seemed to differ little from the "colonization" of the Vietnamese. It was Johnson's successor, Richard Nixon, who reaped most of this anti-Western pap, which took aim at racism, sexism, and capitalism. But this undermining of the nation's creation myth started under Johnson and was directed at Texas and the West he represented. The greatest of all American Western film actors, John Wayne, who bore an uncanny resemblance to LBJ, as if he were LBJ's cinematic doppelganger (or maybe it was the other way around), continued to make patriotic films, including *The Green Berets* (1968), which was not a western allegory but an unabashed and explicit apology for U.S. policy in Vietnam. But other films, such as Sam Pekinpah's *The Wild Bunch*, released in 1969, the year Johnson left office, bid the West farewell in this reprise of the Alamo — a heroic last stand set in Mexico, instead of Texas, and a sacrifice without consequence, point, or meaning. It depicted good, hard men — supernumeraries in a civilized America — who left for a less settled country, where they were swallowed up and forgotten. The point could hardly have been missed by contemporary movie-theater goers.

By March of 1968, Johnson had concluded that the war in Vietnam was unwinnable and started to put in place policies that would allow for U.S. withdrawal, such as "Vietnamization," as it was later termed under Nixon, who would continue this process; Johnson called for negotiations between Washington, Hanoi, and Saigon, which Nixon also continued. Vietnamization, or de-Americanization, meant turning the war over to ARVN — the much maligned Army of the Republic of South Vietnam. Of course, if this army had been an effective fighting force in the first place, there would have been no need for U.S. intervention. Now, ARVN was eventually supposed to do the job the U.S. military had failed to accomplish, which seemed at best unlikely. In the end, ARVN acquitted itself better than expected, but still South Vietnam fell to the North

Vietnamese in 1975. What ARVN did do was provide the United States with a decent interval to stage an orderly withdrawal from the country so that it was the South Vietnamese alone who were left to face the long-awaited invasion from the North.

Johnson's efforts at negotiation would have undoubtedly been more effective had he run for reelection. In the worst decision of his political career, after leaving the Senate in 1960 to serve in the executive branch, he caved in on March 31, 1968, to enormous pressure, pressure from his own party, which foolishly started to abandon him over the war, and pressure from the antiwar movement, which was one-part shrill, one-part silly, one-part substantive, and 100 percent constitutional. Johnson's approval ratings were low, but he had the resources and experience to turn those around if he could have demonstrated to the country that he had a reasonable plan and timetable in place for exiting Vietnam. Instead, he gave Hubert Humphrey, his vice president, who won his party's nomination, the politically difficult, if not impossible, job of running on a record Johnson himself had abandoned. The upshot was that Richard Nixon, the Republican Party nominee, was elected with a plurality of the popular vote — 43.4 percent to Humphrey's 42.7 percent, so still very close results — by telling voters he had a "secret plan" for ending the war. (The vote against Humphrey was much larger, and well over 50 percent, if George Wallace's 13.5 percent is added to the anti-incumbent column.) Nixon had no such plan. Unbelievably, Nixon, for all his cagey intelligence, decided to fight the Vietnam War all over again, but hoping this time for a different result. In this second round, U.S. casualties more than doubled (to fifty-eight thousand), while much more damage was inflicted on Vietnam. The war was even expanded to neighboring Cambodia, with genocidal consequences there. But in the end, U.S. involvement in Vietnam concluded basically on the same terms in 1973 for which Johnson had tried but failed, in his lame duck condition, to negotiate in 1968.

The real tragedy of the Vietnam War was the failure of Johnson, the U.S. commander and chief, to see the war through to the end. His decision to quit before things were finished let down the men in uniform and hurt the country. Clearly, the antiwar movement had succeeded in driving Johnson out of office and helped, indirectly, to elect Richard Nixon. Thus, in the short term, the antiwar movement accomplished little, except to have perpetuated the war for four more long and bloody years. More significantly, the large demonstrations of the Johnson and Nixon years led finally to the replacement of conscription with an all-volunteer service, Nixon's highly effective political answer to solving the military's manpower needs. The hard death of the democratic ideal of shared sacrifice demonstrated that Johnson's problems were not unique to his presidency but indicative of a broader and darker change that had occurred within the very character of the American republic itself. Nixon's all-volunteer service, an institution wisely embraced by every subsequent president, ensured that fighting in the nation's wars would be borne not by a fair cross-section of young citizen-soldiers but disproportionately by the poor and underclass. In short, the reality of the matter was that during the 1960s, many young men who stood to benefit the most from the hard-earned benefits of American society simply became the least willing to fight for them.

If the conflict in Southeast Asia deeply troubled the country and shook the very foundations of the republic, the epic race to the moon reinforced old patterns, and the successful moon landing on July 20, 1969, seemed to vindicate America's destiny as a city upon the hill and as the land of tomorrow. It is to this story of remarkable triumph, and Johnson's crucial role in it, that we now turn.

CHAPTER 7

The Master of Infinity

THE sparkling night skies of the American Southwest, which stretch from LBJ's ranch in the Texas Hill Country to the old missions in Southern California, are special. For much of the year, the desert's perfect pellucid air provides astronomers, and not a few wonder-eyed cowboys, a translucent medium through which to peer above at the canopy of stars. To soar high over the stratosphere would be the only way to obtain clearer views of the celestial kingdom. The Southwest became rightly famous for its starry vault and is today home to many observatories, including the Mount Wilson and Palomar observatories in Southern California, the Kitt Peak National Observatory in Arizona's Baboquivari Mountains, the National Radio Astronomy Observatory, or Very Large Array — a movable radio antenna configured on New Mexico's Plains of San Augustin — and the McDonald Observatory in Texas's Davis Mountains. Indeed, even in pre-Columbian times, dating back to the tenth century A.D., heads were craned back to study the Southwest's night sky, as indicated by the solar and lunar markings at Fajada Butte in Chaco Canyon, New Mexico.

These familiar starlit skies, which had danced overhead since time out of mind, suddenly, on October 4, 1957, looked down with menace. News broke that the Soviet Union had put a satellite, *Sputnik I*, weighing 184 pounds, into earth's orbit. The effect was electric. It was as if a port city awoke one morning to find its ancient avenue to the sea blocked by a vast and unexpected enemy armada. The Soviets possessed nuclear weapons; now it was clear they possessed, or would soon possess, the means to deliver those weapons anywhere on earth. The rockets that launched satellites into orbit were identical with the missiles that could carry nuclear weapons to earth-based targets. In a stroke, then, with the launching of *Sputnik*, the security that America's military forces provided had seemingly evaporated into thin air.

Johnson was at his ranch in Texas that historic day. Typical of his visits home from Washington, he was entertaining guests, giving them in this instance a taste of the Hill Country in fall — a treat indeed. After dinner, Johnson recalled that they went for a walk and "No one said very much. We all walked with eyes lifted skyward, straining to catch a glimpse of that alien object which had been thrust into the outer reaches of our world." Johnson went on: "As we stood on the lonely country road that runs between our house and the Pedernales River, I felt uneasy and apprehensive. In the open West, you learn to live with the sky. It is part of your life. Now, somehow, in some new way, the sky seemed almost alien. I also remember the profound shock of realizing that it might be possible for another nation to achieve technological superiority over this great country of ours."

The story of how the United States found itself in this situation and how Johnson moved decisively to turn things around began in New Mexico, on the far western side of the Llano Estacado. Stargazers may not have been new to the Southwest, but the rocket scientist was. And this not entirely unrelated type first arrived on the scene in the summer of 1930. On July 15, Robert Hutchings Goddard, a pioneer in this new field of research and experimentation, arrived in Roswell, New Mexico, a small town situated in the Pecos River valley. The Goddards rented an adobe house and eight acres, three miles from town, a secluded place called the Mescalero Ranch. Goddard, a college professor, came to New Mexico from Clark University in Massachusetts to continue his work, funded by millionaire Daniel Guggenheim. This support had been obtained through the personal intercession of none other than Charles A. Lindbergh, the famous young aviator whom Johnson had once praised for his bravery and later denounced for his politics. In 1919, the Smithsonian Institution published Goddard's truly path-breaking work, *A Method of Reaching Extreme Altitudes*, and in 1926 Goddard succeeded in launching the first liquid-fueled rocket on his Aunt Effie's farm, near Worcester, Massachusetts, where he was born.

Goddard was an enigmatic man. He tended to be secretive and suspicious of others — and for very good reason. His notion that a rocket could reach the moon was cruelly lambasted by the *New York Times*. This experience in public ridicule taught him to be cautious to a fault and explains, in part, why he withdrew to the Southwest for solitude and peace. It was a place where a person could think. Goddard spent the following years testing his rockets in virtual isolation and far removed from the growing economic depression that was gripping the rest of the country. But he did not withdraw into his work completely.

In 1936, the Smithsonian Institution published Goddard's second great monograph, *Liquid-Propellant Rocket Development*. Goddard's reputation as the father of modern rocketry was secured. In *This New Ocean: The Story of the Space Age*, William E. Burrows makes the compelling argument that many of the pioneering rocket scientists, including the American Goddard, the German Wernher von Braun, and the Russian Sergei Pavlovich Korolyov, were driven not only by the immense technical challenges posed by rocketry but also by the heady dream of space travel. This space-trekking fantasy was nothing new, dating back at least to Johannes Kepler, who believed, "Ships and sails proper for heavenly breezes should be fashioned." Exploring space was an old dream, but one no easier to realize for that. Huge budgets were required to solve the huge technical problems. It was for this reason that rocket scientists turned for support to their respective governments, as Columbus long ago had sought financial backing from Ferdinand and Isabella for his decidedly more terrestrial enterprise. National governments were little inclined, however, to support rocket research until the profound security implications began to dawn on those in power. Once that happened, no expense was spared: the Bolsheviks began investing in rocket research as early as

1921; the Nazis, over a decade later when they came to power in Germany, immediately created a state-supported rocket program; the United States was slow, during the interwar period, to support rocket research, but not as slow as the French. For rocket scientists, this meant that if they wanted to pursue their dreams, they had to strike a Faustian bargain with their respective militaries, with those who would use rockets not to send humans to the heavens but to deliver deadly payloads on enemy targets right here on earth. Indeed, without the prod of war, these visionaries would never have had any hope — in their lifetimes, certainly — of having the resources made available to them to develop the technology to escape the earth's gravity and head spaceward in rocket ships, of witnessing the dawn of the greatest adventure since the Renaissance mariners struck out for new worlds.

In the summer of 1940, after Germany had invaded France, Goddard entertained Homer A. Boushey, Jr. Boushey was a young test pilot and dreamer who a year later would make the first rocket-assisted takeoff of a fixed-wing aircraft (the Ercoupe) for the U.S. Air Corp. Boushey had gained Goddard's confidence, and on this particular warm and starry New Mexican night, out on the veranda, Goddard shared with Boushey the thoughts that lay behind the rocket experiments and his vying for government contracts. According to a shy but irrepressible Boushey, "I remember how hesitant I was about mentioning interplanetary flight" but Goddard "exchanged glances with his wife Esther and then went on to speak not just of travel to the planets, but of interstellar flight as well. He spoke as if it were merely a matter of work and experiments." Goddard, Boushey recalled, speculated that "Future space craft . . . might be equipped with a very light, mirror-like sail. It would be opened up in the vacuum of space like a parasol, and there would be nothing to damage it. It would lock on to the sun's rays, and the energy it received might operate a small boiler which would emit a jet of steam, perhaps, and the ship would sail on and on." Goddard's last years coincided nearly perfectly with the length of the coming world war. In fact, he died on August 10, 1945, the day after the second atomic bomb was dropped from a B-29 Superfortress on the Japanese city Nagasakai.

This new, terrible technology was developed under the same starry sky that had inspired Goddard. A group of scientists, led by the University of California–Berkeley's J. Robert Oppenheimer, lived and worked a couple of hundred miles away in Los Alamos, New Mexico, on the Pajarito Plateau, as part of the Manhattan Project, the origins of which date to 1939 with Albert Einstein's famous warning to President Roosevelt that the Nazis might develop a nuclear fission bomb. Scientists in Los Alamos labored to turn Einstein's famous equation $E = mc^2$ into reality, which they spectacularly accomplished early on the morning of July 16, 1945, at Trinity site, near Alamogordo, west of Roswell. The test's retina-searing success prompted the director, Kenneth Bainbridge, to remark, "Now we are all sons-of-bitches."

At the same time that the scientists in Los Alamos were figuring out how to split atoms over the desert, German rocket scientists had been frantically at work in the German equivalent of Los Alamos, Peenemünde, a facility situated on the Pomerania Coast of the Baltic Sea. There, Wernher von Braun and his team built and tested the V-1 and V-2, Hitler's vengeance weapons—guided missiles tipped with bombs. As the war went from bad to worse, the Nazis removed the rocket program to a location deeper in Germany, a place near Nordhausen in the Harz Mountains. To mass produce the V-1s and V-2s, the Nazis used slave labor, provided by Jews caught in the Holocaust. Thus, the damned were condemned to work and build, under the most vile and wretched conditions imaginable, these new sleek and sophisticated weapons—a vision of one nation's military-industrial complex so awful that it cast a dark shadow on all other efforts. This work produced results, and from 1944 to the end of the war, German missiles rained down on the doomed in Belgium and England. But unlike the atomic bombs the United States used on Japan, these ballistic missiles, if impressive, failed to deliver the knockout blow against Hitler's enemies. Instead of inspiring fear, they inspired envy, and a race was soon on among the Allies to capture German rockets and, better yet, German rocket scientists, including the debonair, handsome, and brilliant Wernher von Braun. In the scramble for spoils, the devil's sorcerer was at the top of everyone's list.

So it happened that after the war, at a place called White Sands, a proving ground in New Mexico that lay a hundred miles west of Goddard's ranch, the United States tested, as part of the Hermes Project, the V-2 rockets it had captured from the Germans. Von Braun and his staff had surrendered to the United States and were transferred from Germany to Fort Bliss, Texas, just south of White Sands. Von Braun remained there until being transferred in 1950 to the army's Redstone Arsenal, located along the Tennessee River, south of Huntsville, Alabama, where he continued his work on rocketry.

With Hitler's cowardly exit from the catastrophe he had caused, and Germany's unconditional surrender, the United States had nothing further to fear from the Fatherland. In the Pacific, Japan's defeat followed soon after Germany's. All of America's dark imaginings, many of them well grounded, were transferred from its vanquished enemies to its erstwhile ally, the Soviet Union, as Uncle Joe morphed into Sinister Stalin. The Soviet Union's successful tests of an atomic bomb in 1949 and a hydrogen bomb in 1953 understandably caused deep anxiety in the United States, just as capitalism's atomic monopoly unnerved the Kremlin. Anxiety turned to panic with the news on October 4, 1957, of the launching of *Sputnik*.

Johnson's troubled musings under that starry sky were soon turned to great political effect once he was back in Washington. His aide George Reedy, a Chicagoan who had joined Johnson's Senate staff in 1951, urged him to use the oversight powers of Congress to investigate *Sputnik* and call into question Republican management of U.S. national security and foreign affairs under Eisenhower, just as the Republicans had called into question the Democratic management of the same under Harry S. Truman six years before. Reedy, according to historian Robert A. Divine in his article "Johnson and the Politics of Space" (1987), was in turn influenced by Charley Brewster, who saw the Soviet achievement as a way to unite the Democratic Party by, in effect, distracting voters from the emotion and controversy over desegregation (the Little Rock crisis had begun one month before). Johnson knew a winning issue when he saw one and took Reedy's advice; he even adopted Reedy's strategic comparisons between the Soviet empire and the Roman and British empires.

In Texas later that month, he gave speeches in Tyler and in Austin, declaring that space was the new "high ground." And just as "the Roman Empire controlled the world because it could build roads," and just as "the British Empire was dominant because it had ships," and just as the United States during the "air age" was "powerful because we had airplanes," the communists, with the launching of *Sputnik*, had "established a foothold in outer space." In more sensational language, Johnson warned, "Soon, the Russians will be dropping bombs on us from space like kids dropping rocks onto cars from freeway overpasses."

With the leadership and help of Senator Richard Russell of Georgia, Johnson revived the Defense Preparedness Subcommittee of the Senate Armed Services Committee and launched an investigation billed as national in purpose rather than partisan. He wanted to score political points, of course, and gain an advantage over fellow Democrats, such as Stuart Symington of Missouri, a potential rival for the Democratic nomination in 1960. But he wanted his investigation to appear evenhanded, constructive, and patriotic. Johnson made it clear that there would be "no 'guilty party' in this inquiry except Joe Stalin and Nikita Khrushchev." And it worked. As Reedy put it, "This may be one of those moments in history when good politics and statesmanship are as close to each other as a hand in a glove." In a matter that had captured the public's attention, Johnson found all eyes were turned to him. He made the most of the situation. Then events conspired to give this moment an even greater sense of urgency and drama. On November 3, one month after the launching of *Sputnik*, the Russians launched a second, bigger satellite, this one with a live dog, Laika, inside.

A month later, on December 6, the United States answered the Soviet challenge with the Vanguard TV-3. While the country watched on their television sets, the Navy's rocket exploded on the launch pad. The incident was perhaps the worst public relations disaster in U.S. history. Two months later, on January 31, the army, which had von Braun on its team, rolled out its Redstone rocket, fitted with a satellite designed by William H. Pickering of Caltech's Jet Propulsion Laboratory. This time the rocket launch achieved its objective. Not only was *Explorer 1* put into orbit, but the U.S satellite made a significant scientific discovery. The instrumentation designed by James van Allen of the University of Iowa detected radiation belts that encircled the earth. The race to space had thus been joined, and humanity's knowledge of the universe and our place in it was about to undergo an intellectual revolution.

In the meantime, Johnson emerged from the hearings as the country's foremost spokesman on space. On the one hand, he warned, "From space, the masters of infinity would have the power to control the earth's weather, to cause drouth and flood, to change the tides and raise the levels of the sea, to divert the gulf stream and change temperature climates to frigid." On the other, he produced a seventeen-point program to ensure that the United States emerged as the preeminent space power. Against this bold call for national leadership, the Eisenhower administration appeared complacent and weak. Through Johnson's skilled efforts, the Democratic Party had appropriated at a crucial juncture the issue of space, allowing them to appear more aggressive than Republicans on matters of defense in the midst of the Cold War and more forward looking in terms of preparing the country to take advantage of space, the new and truly limitless frontier.

In 1924, the same year Johnson graduated from Johnson City High School, Edwin Hubble, at Mount Wilson Observatory in California, discovered that the Milky Way was not the universe, as was once thought, but merely one galaxy among numerous other galaxies; the modern universe, as it turned out, was unbelievably vast, and it followed that possibilities were indeed virtually infinite. This was an interesting fact until the news of *Sputnik* brought home that humans might indeed one day reach the stars. Johnson, who was absorbing everything he could about rockets and space, gushed, "Flights to the moon are just over the threshold." It was one thing for a solitary genius like Goddard, sitting on his veranda under the New Mexico stars, to confide such dreams to kindred spirits. Now, twelve years after Goddard's death, similar dreams were being voiced publicly by the majority leader of the U.S. Senate and to almost universal approval.

Johnson turned the *Sputnik* shock into several major pieces of legislation, which may be seen as the background and context for Johnson's Great Society. Following his National Defense Education Act and the National Aeronautics and Space Act, Alaska was admitted to the Union (Hawaii followed the next year). Unlike the experience of the rest of the territorial West, the admissions of Alaska and Hawaii, as historian John Whitehead has pointed out, were shaped to such an extraordinary extent by foreign policy considerations that the flag's last two stars might well be called the nation's Cold War states, in the same way that the Thirteenth, Fourteenth, and Fifteenth amendments have often been referred to as the Civil War amendments.

Since Abraham Lincoln signed the Morrill Act in 1862 in the midst of the Civil War, and Congress was free of the retarding influence of the Southern delegation, the federal government has played an important role in American education. In the case of the Morrill Act, proceeds from the sale of certain lands from the public domain were to support colleges of agriculture and the mechanical arts and make these institutions more accessible to working class citizens. The result was an unqualified success story, and, indeed, American life would be hard to imagine without the contribution of its land grant colleges and universities. Since 1862, the federal government has continued to democratize and expand educational opportunities, most recently with the passage of the GI Bill of 1944, which provided funds so that World War II veterans could go to college, a program that had a significant effect on the postwar expansion of higher education. And whereas nineteenth-century federal legislation encouraged the teaching of more practical subjects rather than the classics, the National Defense Education Act of 1958 similarly provided federal aid at every level for the teaching of science, mathematics, modern foreign languages, and other subjects, while at the same time respecting the ancient American principle of local control over curriculum in terms of what and when subjects are taught and who teaches them.

The National Aeronautics and Space Act was also a direct response to Cold War imperatives, and given Johnson's big hand in getting this landmark legislation through Congress, he is rightly seen as the "father of NASA." Despite the fact that *Sputnik* was unquestionably the driving event behind this legislation, it was, significantly, not crafted in strictly military terms. Indeed, just as *Sputnik* inspired fear as well as awe, the official U.S. response to the Soviet achievement went well beyond defensive measures. The National Aeronautics and Space Administration (NASA), which succeeded the Wilson-era National Advisory Committee for Aeronautics, was a civilian rather than a military agency, charged with providing for "research into problems of flight within and outside the earth's atmosphere." Furthermore, the act stated it was "the policy of the United States that activities in space should be devoted to peaceful purposes for the benefit of all mankind." This distinction between war and peace invited comparison with President Eisenhower's 1953 "Atoms for Peace" speech before the United Nations, in which he stressed the promise of atomic power rather than its peril to humanity.

Thus, there was a sharp duality to the U.S. space program. On the one hand, it addressed the country's pressing military needs, for as Johnson clearly understood that the American people would not tolerate being second in space or anywhere else for that matter. This position was perfectly in accord with his own competitive, if tempered, nature. Superpower rivalry drove the program, of course, much as earlier national rivalries had driven earlier competing programs of exploration and ex-

President Lyndon B. Johnson with John Glenn, 1965. (George Mason University)

pansion: the Portuguese and the Spanish in the fifteenth and sixteenth centuries or the French and the English in the seventeenth and eighteenth. Each rivalry or age of exploration had its defining gestures and crowning goals: circumnavigating the globe, transcontinental treks, finding the northwest or northeast passages, locating the sources of great rivers, reaching the poles. In 1957, perhaps starting with the successful launching of the dog Laika in *Sputnik II*, the dramatic accomplishment of putting a man on the moon became the great sought-after gesture of the dawning space age.

There were critics, of course, of what appeared to be a new chapter in the old and heroic story of Western civilization's exploration and overseas expansion, except now it was *outer space* expansion and the American West was now a scientific center instead of a scientific frontier. Johnson's fellow Texan the sociologist C. Wright Mills, for instance, was angry at the U.S. reaction to *Sputnik*, which he thought would work to further strengthen the hold of the nation's "power elite" and distract the country from what he thought was more pressing issues at home, a common liberal refrain that the government's priority should always be alms before all else. "Who wants to go to the moon anyway?" Mills snorted. This opposition was relatively small in 1958, when Johnson hammered out the National Defense Education and the National Aeronautics and Space bills, both signed into law by Eisenhower. But over the next ten years, criticism of the U.S. space effort would steadily increase, related to and parallel with the escalating war in Vietnam, which kept the criticism alive with fresh transfusions of urgency and outrage. Eventually, attacks on the Johnson administration would come to include a general critique of Western values. This new anti-intellectualism swept the colleges and universities, turning many of the nation's campuses into centers of protest and dissent. In fact, higher education suffered cannibalistic attacks from within, as students and faculty alike decried it as a tool of power, an extension of the military-industrial complex, and an essentially dehumanizing institution.

Mario Savio was one such disgruntled student. Leader of the Free Speech Movement, he famously denounced, from the steps of Berkeley's Sproul Hall on December 2, 1964, modern education as embodied by the immensely capable Berkeley president Clark Kerr. American education was the envy of the rest of the world, but to Mario Savio and other student radicals, it was something that had to be stopped. In an impassioned speech, in which he yelled more than orated, nearly hyperventilating in the process, Savio declared, "There is a time when the operation of the machine becomes so odious, makes you so sick at heart, that you can't take part; you can't even passively take part, and you've got to put your bodies upon the gears and upon the wheels, upon the levers, upon all the apparatus, and you've got to make it stop. And you've got to indicate to the people who run it, to the people who own it, that unless you're free, the machine will be prevented from working at all!"

A far more balanced view of things, and less melodramatic, came from Charles Percy Snow, an Englishman who in 1959, a year after passage of the National Defense Education and the

National Aeronautics and Space acts, delivered a controversial lecture, "The Two Cultures." In it Snow lamented the estrangement of the sciences and the humanities. Like two great icebergs, they had separated from their common pack and, heedless of the danger, had drifted apart and into ever warmer waters. Snow blamed both sides for failing to understand each other. For it was this gulf, he argued, between the sciences and the humanities that, in part, prevented the West from solving the world's problems, including poverty, which was the real key to winning the Cold War and making the world a better place in which to live.

Although Snow tried to address the shortcomings of both cultures, his most pointed criticisms were aimed at the humanities. He found the intellectuals on this slow bobbing berg ignorant not only of the most basic scientific principles but, worse, seemingly incapable of grasping the critical role the industrial revolution played in improving the lot of mankind. Instead of working to extend the industrial revolution's benefits to everyone, by creating a united culture that embraced science and technology, artists and literary intellectuals had fabricated a nostalgia for a preindustrial age, sneered at consumerism and materialism, held in contempt conformity of any kind, and regarded with suspicion those who would wield power in industrialized states. This was the situation as Snow saw it in his native England. But his analysis was almost immediately applied to the United States, where it provided a good framework for understanding many of the ensuing campus debates.

In the meantime, after Kennedy and Johnson were narrowly elected in 1960, promising the nation a New Frontier, the new president looked for ways to outflank the Russians in space and turned to Johnson. Kennedy had already put Johnson in charge of the space program, making him head of the National Aeronautics and Space Council (created by the National Aeronautics and Space Act). According to Robert Divine, after consulting with Senator Robert S. Kerr of Oklahoma, the vice president turned to James E. Webb to run NASA. Webb had experience running one of Kerr's oil companies and had worked for the Truman administration. More recently, he had served on the Draper Committee, a nonpartisan committee formed by President Eisenhower to analyze U.S. foreign military aid. When Kennedy asked Johnson about the feasibility of putting a man on the moon (he was anxious to beat the Russians, especially after Yuri Gagarin's historic flight), there were very strong people in place to give him an answer.

This was the wrong question, however, based as it was on political rather than technical and scientific considerations. The right question would have been, how can the president better advance the goals of the U.S. space program? And there was, according to Wernher von Braun, a clearly defined program. It included manned orbital flights; building of a space shuttle that could then be used to build an orbiting laboratory and a fixed space station; and then moon and Mars landings. But that said, without the fierce competition that existed between the superpowers, the United States probably would not have furnished the funding for a moon landing as dictated by von Braun's blueprint, opting instead for less expensive, more scientifically justified missions. President Eisenhower, for instance, was not about to "hock his jewels" to send men to the moon. And the *New York Times* and the openly liberal *New Republic* questioned the wisdom and expense of sending men to space.

The pressure Kennedy faced, however, to show Americans that they were not losing the high ground in space increased dramatically after news of Gagarin's path-breaking orbital flight, placing him in the ranks of Magellan. And after the grief the Democrats had given President Eisenhower over *Sputnik* and all the talk of a missile gap, the boldness of a moon landing had great appeal to him. Johnson's report dutifully provided Kennedy with what he wanted to hear, and Kennedy then proceeded to challenge the nation with sending a man to the moon and safely returning him — a goal to be realized before the end of the decade. It was a brilliant instance of presidential leadership, unique in its kind. Kennedy's life was cut short, and the job of seeing through the moon landing fell to Johnson, who steadfastly supported the post-Mercury programs Gemini and

Apollo. The mounting costs of the Vietnam War made this very difficult, but the race to the moon maintained its high priority, even over Johnson's other domestic programs.

Johnson was certainly right that a commitment to making a moon landing "would give," in his words, "dramatic focus to a space program designed to develop our skills and capacities on a broad technological front." And given that on September 19, 1961, NASA announced that a site south of Houston was to be the home of the manned spacecraft center, a $60 million facility (today's Lyndon B. Johnson Space Center), Johnson knew that the U.S. space program would directly benefit the Lone Star State. Robert Divine challenges the suspicion that Johnson pressured NASA to make sure this political plum fell in Texas, but by ensuring that George Brown of Brown & Root, Congressman Albert Thompson of Houston, and the politically astute James E. Webb were all part of the decision-making process, it was all but a foregone conclusion that *Apollo 11*'s long trajectory from the earth to the moon's Sea of Tranquility would start in Texas, even if the launch site itself was at Florida's Cape Canaveral.

According to a memo Webb sent to Johnson on May 23, 1961, Rice University had 3,800 acres of land available to NASA, and the establishment of a major science and engineering center in Houston would make the Southwest as important as New England, with its Harvard and Massachusetts Institute of Technology, and California, with its Caltech and state universities. In short, Johnson may not have had a direct hand in using federal power to modernize Texas and the Southwest in this important regard, but it is doubtful if the city that is Sam Houston's namesake would have become synonymous with the exploration of mankind's final frontier if not for his enormous influence and leadership.

That there was a political side to the space program is hardly surprising. Nor is it surprising that Cold War imperatives and military calculations should have loomed large at the White House, on Capital Hill, and at the Pentagon. But these practical considerations aside, there was also for Johnson an important moral dimension, a classroom lesson in character, to America's space venture, for he saw it as the perfect object of America's can-do spirit. Johnson's hopes that the United States could save South Vietnam were dashed by 1968, but his faith in American technology and know-how was rewarded the following year with Neil Armstrong's famous descent down the ladder of the lunar module the *Eagle*. Johnson, however, saw this incredible technological achievement largely in earth-bound terms. In his memoirs, he wrote, "Space was the platform from which the social revolution of the 1960s was launched. We broke out of far more than the atmosphere with our space program. We escaped from the bonds of inattention and inaction that had gripped the 1950s. New ideas took shape. If we could send a man to the moon, we knew we should be able to send a poor boy to school and to provide decent medical care for the aged." Johnson was absolutely right about Apollo. If Americans could do *that*, what could they not do? But whether this great feat of heart and mind will inspire future generations to their own acts of greatness and courage, terrestrial and otherwise, remains to be seen.

Epilogue
Johnson's Second Mistake

ON March 31, 1968, at 9:00 in the evening, Lyndon Johnson addressed the nation from the Oval Office. The speech was largely about his plans to limit the war in Vietnam, welcome news to a people tired of what had become a military stalemate. Toward the end of his remarks, Johnson surprised the country with the following announcement:

> With America's boys in the fields so far away, with America's future under challenge right here at home, with our hopes and the world's hopes for peace in the balance every day, I do not believe that I should devote an hour or a day of my time to any personal partisan causes or to any duties other than the awesome duties of this office — the Presidency of your country. Accordingly, I shall not seek, and I will not accept, the nomination of my party for another term as your President.

Johnson was one of the nation's great senators. The effect of his tenure in that august body is still felt in his state and his country. His decision to leave the U.S. Senate, where he was master, to run as his party's nominee for vice president was probably a mistake. His presence in the U.S. Senate would have no doubt continued to be as constructive and as stabilizing as it had been during the Eisenhower years. But once in the executive branch, and after the difficult circumstances in which he became president were behind him, he became one of the most accomplished presidents in United States history. Much of the legislation he signed into law remains on the books. And the legacy of his Great Society remains rich and enduring; its efficacy still produces lively debate among scholars and politicians alike. He certainly played a key role in the political integration of southern blacks and the economic diversification of the western estates, thereby bringing to an end de jure segregation and de facto colonialism. The consequences of these regional changes further strengthened and unified the nation as a whole.

And the U.S. space program, a lasting and major success story, which has done so much to advance our knowledge of the world, the solar system, and the universe, would have been a far different thing without his leadership. In fact, his absence is still felt, for no other president has been able to lead in space the way he was able to. And there was his bigger-than-life personality — 100 percent Texan but all American — which captured the imagination of many as well as caused disdain in some. Regardless, Johnson's stamp left an indelible mark on the 1960s.

These many accomplishments notwithstanding, the cares of the presidency wore on Johnson. Despite a lifetime of ambition, when it came down to it, the office Johnson had long sought failed to agree with him. He learned the hard way that being right was not enough. And there was especially the heartache he felt over the war in Vietnam, and the harsh criticism he received because of it. But it is important to remember that he was the last U.S. president to try to prosecute a war by means of conscription, or "the draft" (Nixon inherited Johnson's problem and took steps to move the country to an all-volunteer military.) And for good reason: the nation's attitudes toward honor, duty, and sacrifice had changed. Future commanders-in-chief may ignore Johnson's experience at their peril.

By the spring of 1968, Johnson's approval ratings were down: the war had taken its toll, and the challenges to his renomination by the antiwar and empowerment candidacies of Eugene McCarthy and Robert Kennedy, respectfully, suggested he was losing control of the Democratic Party. This is complete nonsense. The power of incumbency is never to be underestimated, especially when such power is wielded by one with as much political skill and experience as Johnson possessed. It might have been a contentious primary contest, but I believe in the end, a determined LBJ would have carried the day. On Vietnam, he had already indicated that he was looking for an honorable peace, and as president for a second term, he may have been able to secure an agreement earlier rather than later.

This is pure conjecture, of course. But what we do know is that Johnson would not have re-fought the war as Nixon tried to do—with the same result. And what can be said is that if Johnson had decided to stay for another term, this would have significantly altered the political and diplomatic calculus. And just as the power of incumbency would have served him in the primaries, it would also have served him in the general election. As it was, Hubert Humphrey came very close to defeating Richard Nixon, and Humphrey had to run on a record for which LBJ was not willing to run—a very poor hand to play—and Humphrey had to run against George Wallace, a southerner, whom Johnson could have buried. It is thus not too hard to see how a determined LBJ could have remained in office another term.

Again, this is pure conjecture. "What ifs?" are tantalizing questions and make for wonderful parlor games, but they do not make for good history. What is a matter of record is that Johnson was worried about his health, and this was real, and we may infer from his actions that he lost confidence, in the face of so much opposition and outright hostility, to lead. But while the presidency broke Johnson, it did not leave him bitter. He spent his final few years back home obsessing about his ranch, right down to the daily egg count. But he also found time to build a magnificent library in Austin. There were no money worries to trouble his retirement. The Johnsons were rich—even by Texas standards.

Lyndon Johnson died on January 22, 1973. He lived long enough to see the Democrats' antiwar candidate and South Dakotan George McGovern washed away in a tidal wave of voter rejection. The Democratic Party's hard-earned claim to be the party of security and prosperity, hallmarks of the presidencies of Roosevelt, Truman, Kennedy, and Johnson, had been

President Lyndon B. Johnson and Lady Bird Johnson picking wild-flowers near LBJ Ranch, 1968. (LBJ Library, WHPO Collection)

foolishly abandoned, and with it, not surprisingly, the party's long-lived political success. Johnson did not live long enough to learn about Nixon's Watergate scandal. We can only wonder what he would have made of that mess. Johnson was laid to rest not far from where he was born on the Pedernales River in his beloved Hill Country. His wife, Lady Bird Johnson, joined him at the Johnson family cemetery on July 15, 2007. Place mattered to them in death as much as it had in life.

Note on Sources

IN doing research for this biography, I made several trips to the LBJ Library and Museum in Austin, Texas. My most productive visit was made possible by a Moody Grant from the Lyndon B. Johnson Foundation and a Research Award from the University of Missouri–St. Louis. As important as it was to study the Johnson papers firsthand, my experience as a Fulbright Scholar to Vietnam (2001–2002; I arrived one week before the 9/11 terrorist attacks) gave me insights into his years as president that I would never have gained in the archives.

I was able to visit much of the country, Saigon, Danang (the U.S. footprint is still everywhere in evidence in both places), but especially Hanoi and the Red River valley (I spent nine months in Quang Ba, a village outside Hanoi), with the help and assistance of Tran Xaun Thao (of the U.S. Embassy), Nguyen Thanh Hai, and Nguyen Thuy Hang—the latter two of Vietnam National University (VNU) in Hanoi. In addition to teaching U.S. history at VNU Hanoi, I had the opportunity to study under scholars Bui Dinh Thanh of the National Center for Social Sciences and Humanities and Le Van Lan (they participated in an informal study group organized by the Friends of Vietnam Heritage).

I also had the opportunity in 2002 to study Texas history as a participant in Mark Busby's "Traversing Borders: An Interdisciplinary Southwestern Studies Faculty Institute" at Southwest Texas State University in San Marcos (Lyndon Johnson's alma mater), funded by the National Endowment for the Humanities (a Great Society program).

In addition, I had available to me a number of excellent biographies, including those by Paul K. Conkin, Doris Kearns Goodwin, Robert Dallek, Randall B. Woods, and, of course, Robert A. Caro's magisterial work. I found Hal K. Rothman's *LBJ's Texas White House: Our Heart's Home* (2001) particularly useful, as I did *The Johnson*

Years, Volume Two: Vietnam, the Environment, and Science (1987), edited by Robert A. Divine; the oral histories of Joe B. Frantz; and the essays in *The Cold War American West* (1998), which I edited. Students of Lyndon Johnson also have access to numerous published documents and sources, including Johnson's own memoirs, *The Vantage Point: Perspectives of the Presidency, 1963–1969* (1971), and Johnson's White House tapes, several of which have been transcribed and edited by Michael Beschloss in *Reaching for Glory: Lyndon Johnson's Secret White House Tapes, 1964–1965* (2002).

I kept the works by the following authors on the American West, politics, and exploration close at hand: Gerald Nash, Richard Etulain, Michael Malone, Ferenc Szasz, Lewis L. Gould, John Findlay, Donald Worster, Peter Iverson, Richard Griswold Del Castillo, Richard A. Garcia, Richard Lowitt, Stephen Ambrose, Richard White, Walter Nugent, Carl Abbott, Roger Lotchin, Stephen Pyne, and William Burrows; and on the American South: C. Vann Woodward and Howard Rabinowitz. I had the good fortune of taking Rabinowitz's seminar on the South while a graduate student at the University of New Mexico. Of the vast literature on Vietnam, I found William J. Duiker's biography *Ho Chi Minh: A Life* (2000) to be absolutely indispensable. Indeed, I have benefitted greatly from the labors of these and many other scholars, including Bruce J. Schulman and Karen Merrill, who commented on a paper (an earlier version of the Cold War West chapter) I read at the 2004 meeting in Boston of the Organization of American Historians.

Index

CPSIA information can be obtained
at www.ICGtesting.com
Printed in the USA
LVHW090144290619
622761LV00001B/15/P